500 KISSES

 Inventive, tantalizing, and lusty ways to kiss, lick, nibble, and excite the lover in your life!

CIDER MILL PRESS

BOOK PUBLISHERS

Kennebunkport, Maine

13-Digit ISBN: 978-1-60433-138-7
10-Digit ISBN: 1-60433-138-0

This book may be ordered by mail from the publisher. Please include $2.95 for postage and handling.
Please support your local bookseller first!

Books published by Cider Mill Press Book Publishers are available at special discounts for bulk purchases in the United States by
corporations, institutions, and other organizations. For more information, please contact the publisher.

Cider Mill Press Book Publishers
"Where good books are ready for press"
12 Port Farm Road
Kennebunkport, Maine 04046

Visit us on the Web!
www.cidermillpress.com

Design by Melissa Gerber
Typography: Amazone BT Regular, Aphrodite Text R egular, Dalliance Flourishes, Prison AOE, Din Regular, Din Medium
All illustrations courtesy of Shutterstock.com.
Printed in China

1 2 3 4 5 6 7 8 9 0

First Edition

Contents

Introduction

Who said a kiss was just a kiss? Someone who was never *really* kissed! If you've ever been kissed right, your toes curl, your loins rage, and your head spins. Kissing is one of the most erotic acts between lovers. Hungry mouths approach, rising heat draws two bodies closer, hurried hands grope and grab, soft and wet lips part and press against one another, and a juicy tongue slips in and sets you on fire. The mouth is sexy anatomy, made up of sensual parts capable of giving intense sensation and endless pleasure. If you haven't mastered the art of kissing, then you don't know the first thing about sex. Good loving starts with a great smooch. Remember those long make-out sessions with your first love. Hours spent in passionate lip lock. How did we get to the measly one-second peck on the cheek or lips when we grew up? Kissing is magic. You can't get magic in one second. A great kiss is slow and deliberate, long and passionate. A great kisser is skillful, precise, and knows how to spice things up! Do you need to reignite your passion? To reconnect with your partner or create more intimacy? Could an old dog like you use new tricks? Want to jazz up a date night, your wedding night or anniversary, or add excitement to any day of the week or hour of the night? This book gives you 500 mind-blowing, playful, naughty, seductive, and romantic kisses to make your lip-locking sessions sizzle. So grab your partner, keep your clothes on or take them off, and make that soulful connection that kissing creates. By the end of this tantalizing journey, you'll discover (or rediscover) the orgasmic power of the lip and tongue. A kiss will never be just a kiss again!

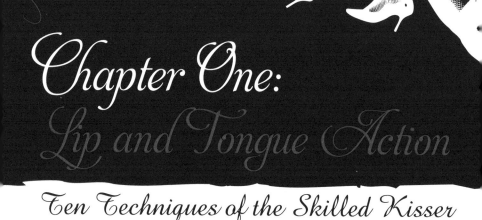

Chapter One:
Lip and Tongue Action

Ten Techniques of the Skilled Kisser

1. Fresh Breath

Clean, refreshed breath is the starting point for a great kiss. Smelly breath repulses, and makes your partner turn their head, or become distant. No one wants to kiss a smelly mouth. Oral hygiene is important. Clean teeth. Cool minty breath. Brushed tongue. And an irresistible smile. When you draw your sweetheart's lips close to yours, an impeccable mouth will be like a magnet.

2. *Juicy Lips*

The kiss begins with the lips, the first contact point between two mouths. Rough, cracked, dry, or peeling lips are no fun to kiss. Who wants to kiss a scratchboard? Moisten you lips with your saliva or a basic lip balm. Ladies, keep in mind that lip gloss or too much lipstick may feel greasy or sticky on your man's lips—not to mention they may also have an unpleasant taste.

Knowing how to use your luscious lips is most important in mastering even the most basic kiss. Lips have the power to give your partner immense pleasure. Their menu of delights includes sucking, caressing, licking, smooching, and nibbling. Pick one or all; the joys are endless.

3. Sexy Eyes

They say it all starts with a look—one that expresses your emotions, the feelings hidden in your heart, your desires. Engage your partner with your eyes, looking deeply into them. Don't lower your eyes. Let them see how much you desire them, how badly you want to kiss every part of their body. When your mouths approach to kiss, keep your eyes open. This creates more intimacy, a moment of deeper connection. Close your eyes now and focus on the kiss, the feel of your lips pressed together, and the movement of your lips and tongue. Stay in sync with each other and let the pull and tug on your mouth set the pace.

4. *Licking*

Licking can be a total turnoff if not done correctly. Who enjoys having their entire face licked? Not seductive. The tongue and its unique texture can give your lover immense pleasure. The catch is being able to control the strokes by applying just the right amount of pressure and saliva on your partner's skin. Final mastery comes from learning how to discover all your tongue's skills. Twist. Twirl. Flicker. Dip. Circle. French kiss. The tongue is a very talented organ!

5. Sucking

A great kisser must also know how to suck. Some of the best kisses involve sucking your partner's lips or a favorite part of their body. It feels orgasmic when there is the right amount of pull on the skin. Sucking too hard is painful. A steady rhythm increases your partner's libido. No need to rush through this. A slow good suck opens up your partner and makes them ripe for plucking.

6. *Tempo*

Each kiss has its own tempo, and within that kiss the tempo can vary. Romantic kisses tend to be softer and slower, picking up intensity as arousal increases. Passionate kisses are faster, the pressure of the lips harder. A sudden increase in tempo can throw off the rhythm of the kiss. Gradually increase or decrease the tempo of your kiss. Make sure you're always in sync with your partner and are able to read their body language and response to your smooches. Remember, it takes two to tango!

7. *Breathing*

Breathing is essential for long, mind-blowing kisses. When you forget to breathe, you run out of steam quickly and start gasping for air or coughing. This definitely ruins the moment. The trick is to remember to breathe! The most common way is through your nose. In the beginning, it may be hard to juggle all the mechanics of lip locking at the same time, but with a steady flow of oxygen, you'll get all the practice you need.

8. Saliva Control

Every great kiss comes with a certain amount of saliva. There's no getting around the exchange of spit. The trick is controlling the amount of saliva you produce when kissing. No one likes a sloppy, gushy, drooling kiss. Yuck! What a turnoff. Moisten your mouth as you start your kiss. As it progresses, you will produce more saliva. Instead of allowing it to collect in your mouth, swallow the excess saliva. You don't want your mouth to be too dry or too wet, but just moist enough for your kiss to feel smooth and fluid. All this lip maneuvering may be frustrating at first, but hang in there. Like bees to honey, with some practice, your lover will keep coming back for more.

9. Frisky Hands

In the midst of a great kiss, don't keep your arms still like a pair of dead fish. While giving a great kiss, use your hands to double the pleasure and stimulate your partner. Squeeze, fondle, rub, and caress your lover's entire body. This shows them just how much you desire and yearn for them.

10. The Art of the Tongue

The tongue has a primary role in French kissing. Making this kiss work is knowing how to adeptly move and place your tongue in your partner's mouth. The mastery of the first nine techniques in this chapter contributes to making this kiss a mind-blowing experience. As you begin, the worst thing you can do is ram your tongue down your partner's throat. This kiss is done in stages. Part your lips. Suck on each other's lips. Slowly slide your tongue in your partner's mouth. Let the tips of your tongue touch and then insert them deeper in your throats. Let your tongues explore and twist around each other. Make sure your teeth don't clash, that you're both in pace with the rhythm of the kiss, and that you don't pull away abruptly. This kiss is the kiss of all kisses when done well!

Chapter Two:
Special Cravings

Kisses That Make You Crave for More

Sweet Kisses

— Lollipop Kiss —

When was the last time you had a sweet cherry lollipop? Think of your partner's lips as the irresistible taste of sugar you've been craving. With no words spoken, slide your hands to the back of your partner's head. Don't look into your partner's eyes. It's all about their luscious lips. Focus on the lips intently. Moisten your lips and inch closer to your lover's mouth. Lick their lips, letting your tongue sweep over the upper lip, and then the bottom one. Take the time to allow them to feel the stroke of your tongue. In between strokes, suck lightly on their lips. Suck. Stroke. Suck. Stroke. Hmm. Tastes good, huh?! After that kiss, you'll be eating candy all the time.

Candy Cane Kiss

The cane-shaped candy stick, often hung on Christmas trees, can be put to much better use. Get cozy with your partner. Unwrap a medium-size candy cane, suck on the bottom end, and look into your partner's eyes. Make sure that look suggests that the party is about to get started. Feel the tang of cool peppermint spread in your mouth. Now, begin by licking the stick, starting from the bottom, traveling up its long spine, curving around the hook—your tongue twisting with the swirls of red and white. Keep your eyes on your partner while showing what gymnastics your tongue can do! Now, it's their turn. Put the candy cane in their mouth, guiding it as they suck and lick on the cane. Let their mouth do all the work. Keep taking turns until the candy cane has melted down or your loins can't stand it anymore.

Turkish Delight Kiss

Called lokum in Turkey, these aromatic confections are an utter delight to the palate. Dusted with icing sugar, they have a plush, jelly-like consistency. Often flavored with rosewater, they come in small cubes—the perfect size to share with your partner. Pick up one of these exotic delights and bite into it, taking only half. Your lips should feel like they're melting against a blanket of softness. Outline your partner's mouth with the other half, leaving a dust of sugar on their lips, and then feed the Turkish delight to them. Now lick the icing sugar off and plant a wet one on your partner, sucking first their lips, and then opening your mouths to taste each other's aromas. Pure bliss!

Hershey Kiss

These bite-size chocolates are perfect for a good smooch any time of the day or night. Keep a bowl of them in the living room, kitchen, bathroom, and, most definitely, in the bedroom. Pick up a Hershey chocolate and place the flat-bottomed part in your mouth, holding it between your lips. Approach your lover's mouth and invite them to smell, lick, kiss, suck on, or bite a piece of the chocolate. Whatever you do, just let it melt into your mouth. You could also pop one of these chocolates in your or your lover's mouth and invite them to taste it as it dissolves on your tongue! There is nothing like chocolate to tickle the senses and ignite the passion.

Fireball Kiss

These spicy, atomic fireballs will surely awaken your partner's palate. Filled with a hot, cinnamon flavor, they will set your mouth on fire. Put one into your lover's mouth and tell them to hold it there. When they can't take the burn any longer, slip your tongue into their mouth to cool things down. Twist your tongue around theirs, suck and pull on it. Use it to steal the fireball away from them. Now, tell your lover to come and get it. Keep passing the candy between both your lips. By now, these candies have spiced up more than your mouths!

Minty Kiss

The taste of mint is one of the most refreshing fragrances for the mouth. It revital-
izes the breath; gives the tongue a tingling, clean sensation; and perfumes your
breath. Pop a peppermint or a mint Tic Tac in your mouth, or brush your teeth with
mint toothpaste. Make sure your lover does the same. Now, draw close together.
Lightly exhale. Feel your partner's cool, minty breath against your face, on your
lips. Suck on each other's lips. Part your lips slightly, and then suck on the tips
of each other's tongue. Take in a little at first. More. Then more. Smell the flavor
and feel the tingle. The heat between the both of you should warm that mint chill!

· Truffle Kiss ·

Truffles are sexy confectionary. Plan a special night with your honey. Create a seductive ambiance: lights turned down low; scented candles flickering nearby; bubbly or wine filled glasses; clothes on, scantily clad, or downright naked; and a box of chocolate truffles. Sink your teeth into the cocoa-dusted, soft chocolate. As the surge of chocolate fills your mouth, invite your Romeo or Juliette to suckle on your lips and tongue. Take a bite of another truffle, and then feed the other half to your lover. Take your time pulling on those lips. Slowly unleash the sensations, and then delve into a mouth full of truffle. Delectable!

•*Caramel Kiss* •

Caramel is so versatile that it can take on many forms in your lover's play. Whether candy, soft dessert, or liquid, the different consistencies can create a load of sensations. The gooey taste of candy coats your lips and fills your mouth with an intoxicating caramel smell. Nibble on those sticky lips, lightly biting down on them as if they were bonbons. Feed your sweetheart a spoonful of caramel pudding or a dripping flan. The creamy custard clings to the palate and soothes the soul. If you want a taste of the caramel sweetness, just feast on your chéri(e)'s mouth. Now, it's time to turn up the temperature. Pour liquid caramel on any part of your beloved's temple. Spread the caramel with your tongue and lick it clean.

Taffy Kiss

There's nothing like the pull of chewy, fluffy taffy between lips. Hold a piece of taffy between your lips, inch closer to your partner, and slip it into their mouth, too. Keep the candy between both your lips and just suck on it like a pacifier. Gently pull on it, both your lips touching each time. How long can the two of you keep your lips wrapped around that juicy taffy? Which one of you has the best lip stamina? As the taffy dissolves, let those sweet juices fall down your chin. After all that lip action, your tongues can take over and get to licking. Who knew that taffy could be so tantalizing!

Bubble Gum Kiss

The pop and smack of bubble gum can be oh so sexy. Take a stick of your favorite gum and share it with your partner. Lodge one half between your teeth, letting the other half stick out like a flap. Invite your darling to bite off the other piece. Chew for a while, and then plant a big wet one on each other. Your mouths should taste like a rush of spearmint, cinnamon, peppermint, etc. Don't be shy. Show your beloved that you each enjoy the flavor. Lock those lips. Intertwine those tongues. Swap bubble gums. Work it!

Kisses with a Zest

～ Strawberry Kiss ～

Strawberries are plucked straight from the menu of erotica. Their plump shape and succulent taste are delightful to many a palate. Put some sweet, bright red strawberries in a bowl. Make sure you take off the green leafy cap. Pop in your favorite slow music, dim the lights, and snuggle up next to your partner. Take a bite. As the flavor fills your mouth, let out a small groan. Lean in close and kiss your lover. The smell of strawberry is aphrodisiacal. You can also outline their lips with the remaining piece and then feed it to them. Take another strawberry and place it between your lips. This time, let your lover bite! If any juices are dripping, use your tongues to lick your skin clean. Yummy!

Cherry Kiss

Simply put, cherries are the lover's fruit. Their dark red pigment enhances their beauty and hints at sweet, fleshy fruit that seduces the palate. Tell your lover to lie down on the bed, on the floor, or across your lap. Take a cherry, wet it in your mouth, and hold the stem between your teeth. Dangle it just above their mouth. Outline their lips, lower it in their mouth and then pull it back up. Lower it. Pull the cherry up again. You're such a tease! Aroused, let them pull the cherry off the stem. Ready to take things to the next level? Take all your clothes off. Place another cherry on any erogenous part of your lover's body. Roll the cherry over that zone with your tongue. Excite your partner until they are panting like a dog. Then take a bite.

Grapevine Kisses

The food of a Goddess Divine, grapes have seductive powers. Clusters of sweet berries sweeten the tongue and awaken sensations. Take a cluster of grapes and pull one off from the woody vines using just your mouth. Hold it on your tongue and draw your partner's face close to yours. As your lips approach and part, slip the grape into your lover's mouth with your tongue. As he bites down slowly and savors the flavor, lick his lips. Want more? Place the cluster of grapes in between your bare breasts. Have your partner eat the grapes one by one until nothing is left. No hands, please!

Bananza Kiss

Before a session of hot and heavy, show your man the pleasures that await him. Slowly peel a banana. When it's peeled halfway, wrap your lips around the banana, slowly descending up and down its length. Keep your eyes on your man. Let him know that foreplay starts in the mind. Take a big bite of your banana. Move closer to your hunk. Start again. Peel the rest of the banana skins all the way down. When you're done loving your banana, move onto your man. Start by taking his shirt off. Kiss his strong torso. Unbuckle his belt. Lightly kiss his stomach. Unbutton his pants. Slip off his boxers or briefs. Kiss his ...

· *Fig Kiss* ·

A fig is a surprising fruit. Its thin outer skin, green and smooth, turns a deep purple as it ripens. Cut open, it reveals a fleshy inside with seeds and a hue of color, ranging from pale yellow to pink, red, and purple. It's only when you taste it that you discover its inner beauty and fragranced juices. Sounds like the female anatomy! Scoop out the inside of a fig and feed it to your lover. Let them first inhale the sweet scent before tasting the ripe flesh. Now you try it. The smell of ripe figs is enticing. When you've finished, start by kissing your partner's neck, leading a trail of kisses to the hidden gems below the surface.

• Honeydew Kiss •

The early morning hour is magical. A silence has fallen over the streets, droplets of dew cling to the surface, and everything seems pure. Take an early walk with your honey before sunset. Stop for a moment and face each other. Time is standing still. Wrap yourselves in the morning dew. Listen to the beat of your hearts and feel the cool moist air against your faces. Press your bodies together and close your eyes. Lightly brush your lips against each other's. Feels like a feather. Now, suck on each other's lips. Tug at the folds of plush flesh. The desire is building. It's time to head back home.

• *Sunkist Kiss* •

A zest of orange with a kiss is a romantic lure from sleep in the morning. While your partner is still in bed snuggled under the covers, peel an orange or tangerine. Orange peels leave an intoxicating scent on your hands that wakes up any sleepy head. Take a bite from an orange wedge. Outline your lover's mouth with it, letting the juices drip over their lips. Tell them to inhale deeply. Hmm, the smell of morning freshness. Gently stick it into their mouth. Splashes of orange wet their tongue. Feed them the rest of the orange and then slip back under the covers with your beloved to finish off what you started.

· *Sanguine Kiss* ·

Love is sanguine, the deepest hue of red. Ruby. Scarlet. Crimson. Almost purple. It's Audacious. Bold. Brazen. Open. Raw. Passionate. Hot-Blooded. Sanguine is a bleeding heart, the blood running through your veins. It's powerful. Enraging. Sexual. Show your lover sanguine colors of your heart. Let them feel every emotion through this kiss. Move in for the kill. Arms open wide, wrap your lover in your arms. Give them a hot kiss on the lips, using all the parts. Lips, tongue, suction. Feast on their mouth. While your mouth is working it, caress their body, using your fingers to make the kiss feel extra special!

· Lychee Kiss ·

Take a trip to the wild side with this exotic fruit from China. It's perfect for cocktails and desserts or eaten as plain fruit. Tonight, you're spicing things up. Create an "ambiance" different from the environment you live in. Prepare finger foods from different parts of the world or a place you loved visiting. Put on some music that transports you to another place. For dessert, lychees will be served. Take off the pink colored rind. Inside, the translucent, pearly white flesh tastes like a sweet, mild fragrance that perfumes your mouth. Pop one into your lover's mouth, allowing them to suck on both the fruit and your finger. Remove your finger. When they have eaten the fruit, a brown nut-like seed remains. Draw your partner near for a kiss. Using the skill of your tongue, take the seed from their mouth. Start again, not stopping until you have gotten your fill.

• Passion Fruit Kiss •

The name of this fruit is just enough to fire up one's hormones. The pulp and juice are highly aromatic. There's nothing understated about passion fruit. Connoisseurs use it in drinks, dishes, sauces, desserts, etc. Lovers can consume it as a starter before the forbidden fruit. Once you cut through the leathery, dark purple skin, scoop up the mouth-watering, juicy interior to gorge on. The taste is so intense that it overpowers the palate. That's how this kiss should be. Irresistible. Uncontrollable. Overwhelming. With a mouth full of flavor, give a kiss that will make your partner's loins will rage.

Let 'em Eat Cake

~ Batter Kiss ~

When was the last time you made a cake with your honey? Just the two of you in the kitchen mixing sugar, flour, and eggs. Get out all the ingredients to make your favorite cake. This is no ordinary cake baking. It's Betty Crocker with a twist. Put on your birthday suits. You heard right. Both you and your partner are going to make that cake in the buck, wearing only an apron. Preheat the oven. Butter the cake pans. Mix all your ingredients. Pour the batter in the cake tin and put it in the oven. Set your timer. Now, start licking the bowl of batter. Use all ten fingers, sticking them in each other's mouths. It's a licking and sucking fest! Wipe your fingers all over each other's bodies and start licking body parts. Feel the temperature rise. By the time the cake is baked, your kitchen should be an inferno!

— *Sugar Kiss* —

Sugar is addictive because it makes the body and soul feel good. It satisfies intense cravings even as you ache for more. It gives comfort and immense pleasure. This is what this kiss is like. So good. Eyeball rolling. Toe curling. Blood racing. Stomach somersaulting. Forget the little pecks on the mouth and cheek. Plant a satisfying, hot one on the mouth. Lick your hottie's lips. Suck on them, one after the other. Slightly open your mouth and give some tongue. More. Open wider, entwining tongues. Wow! They don't say, "Give me some sugar!" for nothing.

• *Red Velvet Kiss* •

The only equivalent to this cake is sex. It's that good. It's naughty and delightfully sinful. Don't be fooled by the angelic, creamy, white icing on the exterior. When you cut into this cake, the interior is flaming red like a brazen scarlet. The moist layers are a bold splash of color, the texture, seductive. Completely irresistible. Prepare a special dessert for your sweetheart. Dim the lights and light some candles. Tell your lover to close their eyes. Cut a piece of red velvet cake and serve it. When they open their eyes, you're standing in front of them naked, holding the cake, with a red bow wrapped around your neck. Slowly feed them the cake, putting some icing on your hands so they can get some licks in. When they're done, straddle your partner so they can feast on you.

Sinful-as-Chocolate Kiss

Pure unadulterated dark chocolate is the ultimate aphrodisiac. "Nourishment of the gods," the Aztecs called it. So creamy it sticks to your skin. For all the chocolate lovers, pour some on your lover's body. Outline the favorite parts of your partner's anatomy. Or start a trail of chocolate from their lips, down their neck, on their chest, down their stomach, in the belly button, ending with the goods. Now, clean up your mess. Divine!

Strawberry Shortcake Kiss

Strawberries. Whipped cream. White cake. The essential ingredients in a strawberry shortcake. Put a piece of strawberry in your mouth and then fill your mouth with whipped cream. Your significant other eats a piece of cake. Bring your mouths together and make your own strawberry shortcake. Feast on each other's mouths over and over again until you've eaten it all. The flavor, the sugar, and the cream should give a rush to set you both on fire.

Ginger Kiss

Did you know that ginger has special mention in the Kama Sutra, one of the oldest texts on the art of love and sexual behavior? In addition to its medicinal uses, ginger has many libidinal properties and is considered a powerful stimulant. It increases blood flow throughout the body, especially to those essential parts needed to give good loving, helping to improve performance and stamina. Give your beloved a whopping dose of ginger before you get it on. Seal it with a kiss. The taste is potent and fiery, but anything that can give a spark to your sex drive has to be powerful!

— Cupcake Kiss —

A good cupcake has been said to be better than sex. Combine sex and a cupcake and it's cosmic.

A cupcake says many things. Sweet love. Small pleasures. Pure bliss. Surprise your partner with a cupcake. Cozy up on the couch or in bed. Feed them morsels while kissing your favorite part of their body. The taste of a good cupcake and the feel of your lips will make your lover heaven bound. Sometimes the sweetest things come in the smallest sizes.

— Dough Kiss —

Kneading dough can rev up your engines. Pulling and squeezing, shaping and molding, and caressing and massaging a doughy mass that resembles human flesh—who knew baking could be such a sexual activity. The next time your honey is kneading dough, surprise them in the kitchen. Stand behind them, snake your arms around, and place your hands over theirs. Kiss their neck and ears, alternating with little bites. Follow the rhythm and movement of their hands. Fingers interlaced, immerse your hands in the dough. Feel the heat generated in your hands. It's a wonder if you're dough ever makes it to the oven!

• Creamy Kiss •

It's time for a magical session of spreading lotion on every part of your lover's body. Arms, torso, back, butt, legs, and feet creamed down with scents that make you want to bite and nibble. Sample body lotions that come in fantasy flavors like chocolate, coconut, cocoa butter, strawberry smoothie, licorice, etc. While you massage the cream in, taste their skin. The smell is irresistible. The taste is decadent.

• *Whipped Cream Kiss* •

My, my, the naughty things you can do with a can of whipped cream. Take a whipped cream shower, generously lathering your lover's body with it. Have an ice cream sundae by spraying your favorite body parts with whipped cream. For example, put dollops of whipped cream on your sweetheart's nipples and add some strawberries or cherries on top. Bon appétit! Make whipped cream undies and then take turns licking them off. Spray some on your fingers and toes and have Romeo lick or suck it off one by one. Fill your Garden of Eden with whip cream and then sit on your lover's face. Call the fire station. By now, I am sure you're bursting into flames.

Parfum Du Jour

— *Vanilla Kiss* —

Vanilla does not have to be bland. The simplest things sometimes give the most joy. This kiss is pure and simple. Soft and delicate. Slow and easy. It makes you feel loved and desired. When your partner least expects it, plant a tender kiss on them. Hold their chin. Look in their eyes. Gently kiss their lips. Look them in the eyes again and kiss them again. Ahh, love is in the air.

~ *Honey Kiss* ~

Give your sweetheart some of your sweet nectar. Dip your finger in a jar of honey and let the honey ooze down your finger. Rub your honey-dipped finger over your partner's mouth and slide it into their mouth. Let them suck off all the honey. Dip your finger in the honey again and this time spread it over your lips. Stick your finger in your mouth and suck it clean. Then ask your baby to lick your lips. As things progress, let the honey drip on any part of your body. Your body is the queen bee and your partner has to work it!

Limón Cello Kiss

As a nightcap, serve up this delicious lemon liqueur to heat things up. It starts out smooth as you take sips of this sweet Italian elixir, but then it adds punch to your palate and fires up passions. That's how this sweet kiss should be. Start out slow and easy. Taste the lemon essence on each other's lips. Pour another round of limón cello. Feel the heat rising, the slow burn, and the rage of your lustful pleasures. Completely intoxicating!

Anise Kiss

Anise is one of the most aromatic herbs. It resembles licorice or fennel in taste and is said to boost sexual desire. Prepare a special anise martini for your chéri(e). In between sips, savor each other's mouth and the spicy fragrance of this herb on your tongues. What a sensuous feeling. As the smell opens your sexual appetite, undress your partner. Pour some of the martini on their skin and suction it up with your lips. That should give your carnal appetite a boost.

Orange Blossom Kiss

Prepare a night of reconnecting with some orange blossom oil and water. Start off with a massage with this fragrant oil. Orange blossom oil is known to soothe and calm and is perfect after a long stressful day apart from your beloved. Take a long hot bath together. Candles, some bubbly, and soft music. After the bath, lie on the bed and take turns rubbing each other down. The stress of the day should be gone by now. Now take a sip of orange blossom water and take turns trickling some in each other's mouth. Let the scent and flavor open up your senses and unlock your libido.

Rose Kiss

Why wait for Valentine's Day, a birthday, or anniversary to send roses to your loved one? A rose is much more symbolic if given to your beloved any time the heart desires. One single rose that says you're the one and only for my heart. Come home with a rose and surprise your sweetheart with it. Let the rose speak for itself. No words, just a kiss to show your love. A sweet, gentle kiss that will moisten her lips and get things started.

Mimosa Kiss

• • •

Start off your lazy Sunday morning with a pitcher of mimosas. Orange juice to awaken the taste buds and champagne (or sparkling wine) to loosen up those inhibitions. As you drink up, give your significant other timid kisses. Kiss your partner on the neck, face, and then finish with smooching each other's lips. No rush. This is just the starting point. Now it's time for bolder kisses that are deeper and more passionate. Slip further under the covers and pull them on top of you.

Saffron Kiss

•••

The sexual benefits of saffron have long been used in tantric sex practices. It is said to be most effective in women as it improves their disposition and increases their sexual desire. Any dish laced with saffron gives it a seductive golden yellow color. Arouse your lady's lust with a meal cooked with saffron. The smell of this spice is distinct and enticing. Everything about this meal should coddle her senses. By the time you're done, your lady will be ripe and ready to be plucked. When you get to the bedroom, suckle on her erogenous zones before you devour every part of her.

• *Jasmine Kiss* •

Everything about this flower is irresistible. Shiny leaves and clusters of attractive white flowers give off a unique fragrance. This beauty of a flower is wildly fragrant and its petals open only at night, closing again in the morning when it's ready to be plucked. Perfume your body with jasmine perfume or oil. Be careful not to put too much on, as it's powerful. One evening, surprise your partner in the buck on your bed. With the alluring scent of jasmine wafting through the air, invite him to come closer. As he approaches, lie back and open your petals. Show him that you can't wait until the morning to be plucked!

• Musk and Amber Kiss •

Strongly diffusive, invasive, making its presence known, musk and amber are very masculine scents. Freshly showered, spray your man's body with his signature scent. Now take your time as you kiss and smell his entire body. This kiss is a sensory lovefest and makes your man feel that there's no part of him that you haven't smelled and tasted. Spin a web of intimacy and explore his body, the dips, folds, muscles, perfections, and imperfections. Claim your territory and make him beg for more.

À La Carte

— Hot 'n' Spicy Kiss —

Turn up the heat! This kiss is for the crazy lovers. Make a selection of food that entices, indulges, challenges, and bombards the palate. This is the time to get out of your comfort zone and try new spices to get your juices flowing. Put on some exotic music ... something reminiscent of a faraway place. Blindfold your partner. Feed them dishes you've prepared, allowing their palate to feast on an array of mouth-watering flavors. Kiss their lips to open up their senses more and increase their desire. By the time you're done, both of you will be ready to travel to another place—the bedroom!

Tequila Kiss

Let loose and plan a night of naughty fun with your partner. It's a party for two. Crank up the music, pull out the tequila, cook up some goodies, and get ready to dance the night away. To shed some of those inhibitions, prepare a shot of tequila. One of you holds the shot glass, the other holds a wedge of lime between the teeth. Take a shot and kiss your partner. Suck on the lime. Muy caliente!

· Frozen Joy Kiss ·

An ice cube is capable of many things. It excites, arouses, tingles, tickles, and makes you shiver. You can pass it along your lover's naked body, lingering around her breasts, stomach, belly button, and privates. The feeling sends orgasmic waves throughout the body. You can just suck on it, passing it between your mouth and your partner's until the mouth-on-mouth action melts the ice cube entirely. You can also outline your lover's lips with it until they're chilled. Then place your hot lips on theirs to warm them back up. The sensation of hot and cold will make you gaga!

· *Ice Cream Kiss* ·

Need a comfort kiss? Something that soothes the soul, quiets the noise of the dizzying world, or allows you to reconnect? Share a pint of your favorite ice cream with your significant other. Block out any other interferences such as music. Turn off your cell phone and the television. Create complete intimacy in each other's company. Feed each other spoonfuls while you alternate between kisses that express your mood. Blissful. Content. Horny. Sensual. Amorous. Greedy. Raw. Vulnerable. Possessive. Don't be afraid to show all your heart's emotions.

• Milkstache Kiss •

A simple glass of milk is not as innocent as you think. Drink some milk and leave the white mustache above your top lip. Tell your lover to lick it off. As they lick it off, slowly suck on his bottom lip. Caress his back, butt, and hips. Inch up to his waste and slowly unbuckle his belt, unbutton his pants, unzip him. Whatever, he has on, take it off in stages. My, my, look what a glass of milk started …

• Sushi Kiss •

This kiss is too hot to trot. Only the daring need apply. Prepare a sake and sushi dinner for your significant other. The only catch is that your body will be the table and your lover will eat on it! Don't let your partner see the "table" before you've set everything up. Place the sushi in key places on your body. To finish off, balance the sake glass on your belly button and the chopsticks between your lips. Don't move. Hold it. Now, shout out to your lover, "Dinner is served!"

• Popsicle Kiss •

Orange. Grape. Strawberry. Cherry. So many fun flavors to play with. On a hot summer's day or night when it's almost one hundred degrees in the shade and you can't keep your clothes on, cool down with a popsicle. Take turns sucking on that ice pop, licking and sliding it against each other's hot flesh. Feel the cool chill on your skin, the swirl of a cold tongue, or the pressing of frosty lips on your nipples. Brrrrr!

Chocolate and Champagne Kiss

Set out some of the finest chocolate and chill your favorite champagne. When your lover sees this arrangement, they should understand it's time for some loving. Chocolate and champagne are made for lovers. The melting of pure bliss on your tongue and the burst of effervescence in your mouth are more than enough to set the tone and get you in the mood for love!

· Breakfast in Bed Kiss ·

Prepare a copious breakfast for your sweetheart after a night of hot lovemaking. All that love should have given you both a ravenous appetite. Strawberries, cherries, passion fruit, or figs. Freshly squeezed orange juice. Pancakes oozing with syrup, topped with whipped cream. Sausages and eggs over easy. This is breakfast for a king and a queen. Satisfy each other's appetite with food and kisses. Eat. Drink. Kiss. Lick. Suck. By the time you're done, you'll have energy for another round of love.

· Oyster Kiss ·

Oysters are natural Viagra. Rich in zinc, it's believed that they do wonders for the male libido. Prepare a tray of oysters. Throw in some bubbly to loosen things up! Eat an oyster. Bring it close to your lips and show your man how it's eaten. Tell him how fresh and pure the juices taste and how soft and delicate it feels in your mouth. Let out a long groan as it goes down your throat. Now that you've shown him how it's done, feed your man an oyster and let him taste what he's been missing. Keep feeding him as many oysters until he's filled with enough mineral to keep his stamina for the rest of the night's oral pleasures!

Chapter Three:
Kiss Anatomy

Lips Aren't the Only Parts That Need Kissing

Head and Neck

— Hair Kiss —

There's nothing like a slight pull of the hair that turns the sexual tension up a notch. It makes you feel desired and craved by your lover. Starting from their hairline, seep your hands into their hair and pull their head back. The gentle, yet firm tug will excite them. Look into your lover's eyes and come in closer. Your lips are so close, but not yet touching. Hold it. Now kiss your lover's lips. Move their head back and forth in a steady rhythm, tasting their lips each time. Make your partner lust for more, and as you build the desire, tighten the hold of their hair. You have them just where you want them.

~ Lobe Kiss ~

The earlobe is one of the most sensitive erogenous zones. Tickled or suckled right, sensations of the unspeakable kind rush through your body. This kiss can be done in just about any kind of position, but the feeling becomes orgasmic when you pull on that lobe from behind. Stand or kneel down behind your partner. Snake your arms around your lover's torso and caress their chest. Let them feel your breath hitting the back of their neck. A tingling sensation creeps up the spine. Take your partner's earlobe into your mouth and tug on it gently. Vary your lip action. Kiss. Nibble. Lick. Suck. Swirl your tongue around it. Ooh la la. At this point, your partner should be purring like a kitty!

· *Ear Kiss* ·

This kiss takes some skill. No one likes a wet tongue rammed down their ear. Lead into this kiss by first nibbling your partner's neck, traveling up the side of their neck. Suck on their lobe, which by now you've mastered. Outline their ear with your tongue, letting them feel every tingle of sensation. Take your time inserting your tongue in their ear and make sure there's not too much saliva. Let the contact of your tongue create a whirl of frenzy buzzing in your lover's ear.

Upper Lip

This kiss definitely gets things started. Start off with a kiss on your partner's lips. Nothing fancy, just a simple kiss. Then moisten their lips with your tongue. Pause and look at their lips. Place your hands on their booty. Draw them closer so you can feel the movement of their body against yours. Lightly kiss your lover across the top lip. Now fully take it in your mouth, sucking on it like pacifier. Press your mid sections against each other to show just how much you're enjoying it.

Bottom Lip Kiss

This kiss is a great prelude to the main course. Begin with a trail of kisses from your partner's bellybutton, stomach, up their chest, neck, ending at their chin. Lick their bottom lip, and then bite down on yours. Suck their lip, slow and steady, gyrating those hips. Feels good, real good. Don't stop pulling on it until both of you explode!

Neck Kiss

This kiss makes your toes curl. Run your tongue up and down your partner's neck. Swirl, flicker, and twist it against their skin, creating a frenzy of excitement. Then lightly kiss their neck in different places. Settle on a spot. Bite down while squeezing a favorite part of your lover's body. Settle on another spot. Bite and squeeze. Alternate the tongue, lip, and teeth action. The pressure is mounting and the heat is rising. Now it's time to rip off each other's clothes.

Nape Kiss

This is another spot made for kisses. Undress your partner and let them remain standing in front of you. Move behind them and grab their chest. Kiss their nape, moving your lips quickly in a steady rhythm up and down the back of their neck. Lick their neck and lightly blow on it. Feels so good! Add some tongue action now. Move your hands down their chest until you find the gems. This should make them surrender!

Jugular Notch Kiss

• • •

There's a hollow, a dip at the base of the neck, that's sexy and inviting. It's a secret place with undiscovered pleasures. Put your lips in this space on your lover's neck and claim it. Follow the dip with your tongue. Outline it with your fingertips. Smell, suck, and lick it. Discover new sensations hidden in your body.

~ Collarbone Kiss ~

This kiss is most enjoyable with your partner backed up against a wall. Undress your lover. Lightly run your fingers along their collarbone. Kiss and lick along the collarbone, sucking from time to time. As you continue to kiss it, grab your lover's hips and press them firmly against your mid section. Change the placement of the hands and caress different parts of their body to let your partner know that you're about to spice things up.

• Areola Kiss •

Before you get to that sweet nipple, have fun in the pigmented area surrounding it. Twirl your tongue around it. Lick it clockwise. Counterclockwise. Focusing solely on that zone, kiss it and squeeze her breasts. The trick is avoiding the nipples. Mastering this kiss depends on the placement and tempo of the tongue. Done right, it gets your baby revved up for the main course.

· Nipple Kiss ·

This kiss is on the top ten mind-blowing list. The sensations are wild, a must have on any woman's list. Hold your lover's arms up while you feast on each nipple. She's your prisoner! Lick and blow on them. The cool air against her nipples will spark her excitement. Now suck on them, sinking your lips into her plush bosom. Let you lips sweep across her peaks. Change the direction of your tongue. Pick up the momentum between your sucking and licking. Drive your honey wild and leave her gasping for air.

• Brassiere Kiss •

Instead of her bra, your sweetheart can wear your kisses. Slip your fingers under the bra straps and pull it off the shoulders, giving your lady light kisses where the straps used to be. Unfasten the clasp and press your lips lightly against her back. Continue around to her breasts and smother them in kisses.

· Deodorant Kiss ·

Lift your partner's arms above their head. Nestle in the hollow of their armpit. Inhale deeply, taking in their scent, and breathe out. The heat from your mouth makes your partner's temperature rise. Interlace your fingers with their hands and kiss them along the armpit. Inch up their inner arm and lightly bite the soft skin. Let go of their hands when you're ready to devour them.

Shoulder Kiss

This kiss is very sensual and definitely gets your partner in the mood for love. Stand in front of a mirror, your partner in front you. Expose her shoulder and let your fingers graze its curve. Look into her eyes through the mirror's reflection. Make your desire apparent. Kiss her shoulder while you caress the rest of her arm or breasts. Vary the pressure of your lips and alternate between kisses and licks. Move to the other shoulder and turn things up a notch.

· Button Kiss ·

The bellybutton was made for sexual play. Whether an "outie" or an "innie," licked, sucked, or kissed just right, it tickles and excites your partner endlessly. Kiss around it. Dip your tongue in or twirl your tongue around it. Fondle it. Suck on it. Put whipped cream on it and lick it up. Or when your baby comes home at night, lift up their shirt and slowly kiss their belly, ending in the center at their navel. Pull their shirt down, take their hand, and lead them into the bedroom. Don't forget to put the "Do Not Disturb" sign on your door!

Back Kiss

A naked back is beautiful anatomy. The slope and curve of skin and muscle is perfect terrain for kisses. Have your lover lie on their stomach. Straddle your partner or lie down on them. Trail kisses along their back from the lower back to the neck and vice versa. Alternate with soft love bites. Lick their back, swirling your tongue along the contours. Breathe lightly over their skin to give them shivers. When you're done feasting, turn them over for dessert.

• Lower Back Kiss •

While you and your lover are in bed, your body toppled on theirs, dazed in the afterglow of sex, turn your partner around and lightly kiss their lower back. Take your time. Make it nice and easy. The light kisses on the lower back will slowly replenish their desire and build their energy back up for another round.

Love Handles Kiss

While standing up, lips locked in a hot smooch session, or in bed in the climatic throes of passion, grab onto your lover's love handles to bring them closer. A firm yet gentle grip stakes your claim and increases intimacy. While holding those handles, kiss your partner passionately. Love and desire are not bashful and have no hang-ups. Show your lover that you want every part of their body, even the extra padding that allows you to hold them in a way to give more loving.

Below the Belt

~ Inner Thigh Kiss ~

This kiss is a prelude to some sexual healing. Spread your partner's legs (or hook one of her legs over your shoulder). Lightly kiss her inner thigh, starting from the knee to her crotch. Get your lover's juices flowing with lip and tongue action that varies. Slow licks that drag over her skin. The flutter of your tongue. The pull of hungry lips. Small spasms begin to take hold of your lover's body, her legs shake, and moans jumble in her throat!

~ *Lap Kiss* ~

This kiss seems innocent, but it's downright mischievous. Undress your lover and sit him down on the edge of the bed. Caress his lap, your hands moving in a sweeping motion. Take your time, sometimes sucking, licking, and nibbling on his skin. When each leg has gotten its due, look up at your lover and smile coyly. Now gently push him back on the bed, suggesting that you're about to dine on the goods!

• Fuzzy Kiss •

The Garden of Eden holds many secrets. Snake your tongue through the warmth of your lover's garden. The taste and smell of their oasis will excite you. Vary the pressure of your lips and the tempo of your tongue. Tease them mercilessly, stopping each time before you unlock the treasure.

Down Under Kiss

This kiss is a trip to the wild side. One of the most orgasmic kisses, it takes a skilled kisser to unleash all the pleasures that this kiss can give. It takes a bold tongue and a voracious appetite to master this kiss. The entire mouth is at the service of pleasuring your lover. All parts are moving, lips, tongue, and hands. Add a balanced dose of sucking, licking, and kissing and your lover's body will become putty in your hands, or should I say mouth!

Booty Kiss

The luscious booty merits its own set of kisses. It's usually fondled, grabbed, spanked, but not kissed enough. In the shower, in bed, or anyplace where the urge finds you, hold onto your lover's hips and bite gently on her buttocks. Suck and lick on her humps, swaying her hips to your tongue's cadence. Place kisses on each cheek and let out a long groan of pleasure. There's nothing like savoring a supreme piece of booty. Smoking hot!

Knee-Buckling Kiss

A proper kiss makes you weak in the knees. Surprise your lover from behind. Tell her to close her eyes. Take off her top as well as yours. Enjoy the skin-on-skin contact as you run your fingers along the contours of your partner's torso. It feels like sparks are popping on your skin. Fondle her chest and squeeze her nipples as you kiss and suck on her neck, creating a frenzy of sensation. After the first buckle of her knees, you won't be standing for long.

Arm's Length Kiss

Extend your partner's arm and caress it. Smother their entire arm in kisses—triceps, biceps, and the inner arm. Inhale deeply. Lick and blow. Kiss and suck. Alternate between long strokes and swirls of tongue. Make sure you give that arm a hot workout!

Back of Leg Kisses

• • •

Flip your partner around on the bed. Start from the waist down with warm kisses along the back of their leg, continuing up the other. Gently bite down in certain places to increase arousal. Your lover's desire slowly peaks and opens up their libido. Let the rest of the party begin!

Loose Ends

~ Thumb Suck Kiss ~

This kiss is many things. Naughty. Suggestive. Animal. Vulnerable. As you begin foreplay, this kiss will give your lover a taste of things to come. Dip your thumb in their mouth. You're in control here, so set the rhythm. Let them suck on your thumb as you insert it deeper in their mouth. Slide your finger in and out of their mouth, stopping at the tip each time. Look into each other's eyes the entire time. This is what I call finger-licking loving.

Pinkie Kiss

This kiss is code for "Let's get it on!" Without any warning, grab your partner's hand and lift up their pinkie. Insert the tip in your mouth and circle it with your tongue. Then suck on it, taking it deeply into your mouth. Slide it along your tongue and pleasure their pinkie as long as you want. Your lover should get the hint after that.

Hand Kiss

Who said that gallantry was a thing of the past? This kiss is classic, a timeless gesture of love. It should be spontaneous and carefree. Walking down the street, strolling in the park, having breakfast or dinner, or lying in silence in a moonlit room, take you lover's hand and give it a simple kiss. This one kiss says everything that's in your heart.

· Knuckle Kiss ·

This kiss gives your partner ten times the pleasure. Ten knuckles. Ten kisses. Suck on each knuckle. Pucker those juicy lips and give each knuckle the love it deserves. As you move from each knuckle, spice things up. You've learned a few tricks thus far to show your partner what your lips are capable of doing. Don't stop until you get to ten.

· Palm Kiss ·

This kiss is even more pleasurable when it's combined with a hot session of sex. As the passion intensifies, take each other's hands. Your heart is beating fast, every nerve in your body is sensitive, and your thrusts get deeper. Suck and bite the palm of their hand. Bite as hard as your partner can take it followed by kisses and licks. Exhale so you both feel the fire from inside. At this point, you're turned from the inside out and about to burst into flames.

• Toes Galore Kiss •

Have you ever had your feet washed? It's one of the most erotic experiences you could ever give your lover. Fill a basin of warm water with your favorite aromatic oils. Immerse each foot in water, caressing their entire foot underwater and cascading water over it. When you're done with the first part of this ritual, suck on each toe, keeping your eyes on your sweetheart. The pleasure of watching the pull of their lips, of feeling the suction of your mouth, and the slide of your tongue on their toes is pure seduction.

• *Foot Fetish Kiss* •

Feet also have many talents. As you sit across from each other, pleasure your lover using just your feet. No hands! Caress each other's feet, intertwining them. Or run your foot up your partner's leg, circle their nipples with your toes, and tickle their private parts. Toes have the power to delight, too!

• Arch Kiss •

The most ticklish part of the foot is the arch. Take your partner's foot and place your lips in the arch. Breathe deeply to awaken their sensations. Press your lips against their arch, part your mouth. Move your tongue in a sweeping motion along their arch and alternate with long sucks. The feeling is orgasmic.

• Ankle Kiss •

After a long day of work, sit your partner down on the couch and serve them a glass of wine. Pull off their shoes and socks to massage their feet. When you're done with each foot, give each ankle a bunch of kisses. Their stress and worries of the day will melt away and put them in the mood for a night of love.

Wrist Kiss

Wear a bracelet of kisses around your wrist. Circle your partner's wrist with feather-like kisses. Start again, but this time suck on their skin as you go around. As you begin to circle their wrist for a third time, use the tip of your tongue to spice things up!

Random Parts

— Hairline Kiss —

This kiss is simple, yet it reinforces the intimacy and connection between two people. Hold your partner in your arms. Look deeply into their eyes and then kiss them along their hairline, from ear to ear. While giving kisses, you can run your hands through their hair and hold their head back for more sensation. This kiss has a slow tempo. Each given kiss should feel light, warm, and deliberate. This kiss expresses many things. Love. Happiness. My one and only.

Eyebrow Kiss

This is another sweet kiss that displays the love between a couple. Plant tender kisses on your partner's eyebrows while you run your hands up and down their back. Let them feel the warmth of your breath on their brow. Feels like bliss!

Nose Kiss

This kiss is romantic and doesn't have to involve lips. Snuggle under the covers with your partner. Bring your faces close, noses touching. Close your eyes and rub your noses together. While your noses are cuddling, let your moist lips brush against each other. That should add some sparks!

• *Mascara Kiss* •

This kiss sends a flurry of sensation through your partner. While your partner sleeps, give them a kiss on their eyelashes. For this kiss to feel enjoyable, they should be barely touching your partner's lashes. Your kiss should feel feather like, only creating a light tickle. If your partner starts to stir, give them another kiss until they slowly open their eyes. Now that they're up, have your way with them!

• *Dimple Kiss* •

Dimples are sexy. They make a smile irresistible. No wonder you can't keep your lips off them. Hold you sweetheart's face in your hands and plant a kiss in their indentation. Suck on it and dip the tip on your tongue in it. The key to this kiss is the pace and the pressure of your lips. Too much can be a turnoff in this area. So take it nice and easy. Combine this kiss with caresses that will set your baby on fire.

Chin Kiss

This kiss is suggestive. It seems innocent, but it's definitely on the risqué side. Position yourself so you're at the level of your partner's chin. Start off by giving it light kisses. After that, hold onto their hips and suck their chin, pulling gently on it. Keep a slow and steady pace to wake up their libido.

Heart Kiss

This kiss is loving and one of the most tender. Take off your partner's top. Rest your head on your partner's bare chest. Place your ear on their heart and listen to the beat. Turn your face around again and give them kisses in the middle of their chest. Start off slow, and then increase the pressure of your lips. Alternate with licks, starting from their heart down to their bellybutton and continuing back up. Finish off the kiss by resting your head on their chest again, listening to the beat of their heart.

Elbow Kiss

This kiss is perfect for an afternoon of tasting each other's pleasures between the sheets. Straddle your partner and grab their wrists. Pull their hands over their head and bend down as if you're about to give a kiss. Get close enough that you're lips are almost touching. Feel each other's breath, look deeply into each other's eyes. Pucker your lips and when they almost brush against each other, pull away and take their elbow slowly in your mouth and suck on it. Suck on the other one. When your lips have whet their appetite, move on to the main course.

Spinal Tap Kiss

This kiss will have your lover's body in spasms. Flip your partner's naked body around and kiss them down their spine. Kiss, lightly suck, and lick. Repeat the kiss, but add some whipped cream along their spine. Now, eat and lick it off. Start again with an ice cube. Run it slowly along their spine. By time you're done with them, they'll be screaming for mercy.

Back of Knee Kiss

• • •

Often overlooked, this is area is highly sensitive. Strummed the right way, it makes your lover sing your praises. Lie you partner facedown on the bed or floor. Kiss the back of their knee lightly, sucking alternately. Lick playfully and then blow on your saliva. Fondle that spot with your finger. It will tickle and excite your partner. If your sweetheart is standing up while you're giving them this kiss, they'll become week in the knees!

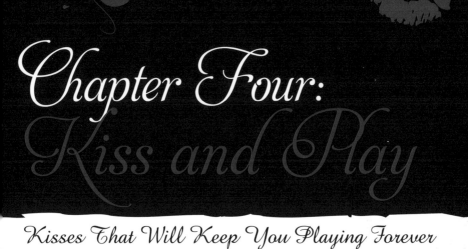

Chapter Four:
Kiss and Play

Kisses That Will Keep You Playing Forever

Gaming for Kisses

~ Hide and Seek Kiss ~

Get ready for a playful night of sex! Stand naked in front of each other in the bedroom, and both of you put on blindfolds. Turn off the lights and separate. One person starts off first and tries to find where their partner is in the dark. As you become more sensitive to sound, grope your way through the dark until you feel your partner. Touching hands, pull them close and kiss. The first kiss should be simple. As you take turns, the kisses slowly become passionate as your senses heighten, and your passion unleashes!

Peek-a-Boo Kiss

This kiss is sensual and inviting. It invites your partner to discover parts of your body and give them pleasure. Lying in bed, cover your nude breasts with your hands. Let your lover move your hands to give you an areola or nipple kiss. When you're ready for more, hide your pubic area this time and let your lover pry your hands away. Now it's his turn. Play peek-a-boo until you've unlocked all your desires.

Blind Man's Bluff Kiss

Get out the blindfolds again. Only one partner is blindfolded this time. Both of you are in the nude. One person hides somewhere in the house while the blindfolded lover tries to find them. As they grope their way to you, give hints, throw them off track, or tease them. Arouse them a little with light kisses and touches and then go back to your hiding place. Lure them to you slowly and when they finally find you, tag them with kisses.

· Kiss and Tell Kiss ·

Imagine the most mind-blowing, earth-shattering, eye-popping kiss. Share it with your lover and ask him to give you that kiss. This kiss is not the peck on the cheek or lips, a basic smooch, or even the delightful French kiss. This kiss is a four-course meal, feasted on in stages. The first kiss opens your palate. The second kiss makes you crave for more. The third kiss begins to fill every part of you and satisfies your hungry desire. The last kiss tops you off!

• Simon Says Kiss •

"Your wish is my command." Whatever kiss your partner desires shall be given. Choose your most favorite kisses and tell your partner to give you some lip action. Nothing is off-limits and every wish will be granted. Now it's your lover's turn. How far will you go? How naughty will you be?

· Twister Kiss ·

Set out a game of Twister on the floor. Rules of the game: All players are naked. Each time a player spins a color, the other one places their hand or foot on the corresponding color and gives a kiss. As the game progresses and your bodies rub, touch, and contort in crazy positions, the first person who falls must give the winner a victor kiss they'll never forget!

· Bull's-Eye Kiss ·

This kiss is great for jump-starting your libido. Pick a part of your body as the main target. It can be your lips, your breasts, or your booty. Have your lover kiss his way to the main target. Each kiss should arouse and excite, with lip and tongue efforts more ardent as he gets closer. By the time he gets to the bull's-eye, you should be on fire.

• Poker Kiss •

Players are in the buck. Cards are shuffled, cut, and dealt. Bets are on. Game begins. No chips. Kisses will raise the stakes. Each time a player has to fold a round, the winner of the round marks down a favorite kiss they want. By the final round, the winner takes the jackpot and gets all the kisses.

· Karaoke Kiss ·

Get out your favorite playlist, crank up the music, and start jamming. It's a night for dancing. Play all your hits, the songs that express your heart's emotions. Shake your booty. Move your hips. Swirl and twirl. Give your partner a lap dance. End each song with a sweet, erotic, sensual, or downright horny kiss that lets them know just how much you feel about them.

· Charades Kiss ·

How well do you know your kisses? Act out your favorite kisses. Blindfold your partner and undress them. After you give them a kiss, they have to try to guess which kiss it is. If your guess is right, your next kiss will turn up the fire. If they guess wrong, all your partner gets is a measly peck. The object of the game is to get the fire blazing!

Costume Party for Two

～ Candy Striper Kiss ～

Surprise your man in a cute red and white candy striper outfit. Sashay over to him and tell him that you want to make him feel better and you know the perfect remedy. Take off his clothes, kissing and sucking his naked skin each time an article of clothing comes off. When he's completely undressed, sit him down in a chair. Straddle your partner and give him a kiss that will melt away all his ailments.

French Maid Kiss

When your man comes home, greet him in a sexy French maid costume. You're at his beck and call tonight. Serve him a cool cocktail. Feed him a spicy dinner. Draw a hot bath and bathe him. Dripping wet, lead him into the bedroom and lay him on the bed. Get on top and kiss him timidly at first. As you continue to suckle on his lips, make your kisses more passionate. The heat from your lip action will dry his skin.

~ *Vampire Kiss* ~

This kiss will claim you for eternity. Tilt your lover's neck to the side and suck on it. Tug firmly on their skin, making a red mark. The taste of their skin makes you hungrier and more insatiable. It's feeding time. Bite their neck firmly, but not too hard. As you bite down, alternate with full juicy kisses. You'll possess them forever!

Lolita Kiss

This kiss is red-hot seduction. Use your seductive powers to turn on your lover. Create an erotic ambiance. Racy lingerie, handcuffs, a bubble bath, or massage. This kiss involves mostly sucking and licking. Feast on your man's entire body, from head to toe. Seduce him with your lips and show him what wonders they can do!

Night Nurse Kiss

The night nurse's kisses will raise your temperature. With his eyes are closed or when he least expects it, give him kisses that make his heart beat faster. Specialize in kiss anatomy and become quite knowledgeable about the healing properties of kisses on the anatomy. Start out with small dosages at first, but as his body heat rises, his pulse races, and his breathe becomes short, increase the amount until you put him out of his misery!

Hercules Kiss

There's nothing like a man who knows how to handle business. Strong arms packed with muscle. Bulging pecs. Sturdy hands. Strength is a quality that will turn on any woman. Swoop your honey in your arms and take her to the bedroom. You can also pick her up and let her legs straddle you. As you carry her, give her hot kisses that make her impatient for the pleasure that awaits.

• Cat Woman Kiss •

Svelte, feline creature. Sensuous. Secret. Playful. Mysterious. Let the sexy cat woman in you lure your lover man to your boudoir. If you feel daring, get into costume to feed his imagination. Wear cat ears, seductive black lingerie, and draw whiskers on your nose. While you undress your man, smell his skin and lick to taste. Purr to let him know that he smells and tastes so good. When you finally get him in bed, continue to taste his entire body. By the time you're done, he'll be purring just like kitty.

Samson and Delilah Kiss

The male anatomy is perfection, a work of art to feast on. The caress of your hands and the desire in your eyes are the foundation of this kiss. Explore every part of your man with your hands. Kiss the strongest parts of his body, those that make him the most sexy to you. Show him with your hands and eyes that you admire his strength. He should feel in your kisses how much he turns you on. Make him weak with your kisses. When you have him just where you want him, overpower him with your secret weapon.

Wonder Woman Kiss

You're powerful and strong, yet soft and bashful. You won't blink to fight the forces of evil, but you're vulnerable and, at times, weak. You have a heart that loves many, but only a special place for one. You're his wonder woman and your kisses bind him to your heart. Spin your lasso and trap your man in your arms for the night. It's been long overdue, a session of hot and heavy! No sex, just kissing, sucking, licking, petting, and caressing!

Superman Kiss

Surprise your sweetheart with a special night—dimmed lights, candles, flowers, jazzy music, a glass of wine, and a three course meal. Wine, dine, and kiss her during the entire time. The kisses should be tender and romantic, sweet enough to rouse her passion. After dessert, spice up your kisses and put the heat on full blast! You know a few tricks by now. Give her the toe curling kisses. Show your lady that not only does she have a man who knows his way around the kitchen, but one who also knows how to satisfy her. You'll always be Superman in her eyes!

A Second Life

• Swept Away Kiss •

Picture this: an empty beach, warm sand under your feet, the lulling sound of the lap of the ocean, and a beautiful full moon lighting your path ... Utopia! Take an overdue vacation with your significant other, a place where there's miles and miles of deserted beach. It's time to deepen your intimacy and reconnect. One night during your trip, take a stroll on the beach. Start kissing each other passionately and fall to the sand. Roll around in the sand while you feast on each other's mouths. Think of nothing else but those fiery kisses. For one night, you're shipwrecked lovers on a desert island.

Strangers in the Night Kiss

Plan a meeting place with your partner in public. It can be on a bridge, a park bench, next to a fountain. You're complete strangers and cross paths suddenly. The attraction is immediate. You approach slowly and smile nervously. Your bodies come closer. Your heartbeat races, your breath slightly labored. The emotion overwhelms you. Your lips press together, hard, and your mouths are eager, hungry. Your hands grope each other's bodies hurriedly. Life continues around you, but both of you are oblivious. When your passions ignite, take the party behind closed doors!

Courtesan Kiss

Offer your man an entire night of your charms and sexual pleasures. Turn your bedroom into a love harem and lock him in there for the night. Seduce him in stages. Show him the orgasmic marvels of your tongue, teeth, lips, and then your hands. You could have written the Kama Sutra and then some. This is a night to set your love on fire. Take your time. You have until sunset!

Talented Mr. Ripley Kiss

This kiss is for the imaginative. Get into a sexy character and surprise your lady. Greet her as a double agent in a suit, a French waiter wearing just an apron, a policeman with handcuffs, a fireman with a hose, or a handyman in just a tool belt. Don't be shy and have fun. Your kisses should be representative of your character's charms. The key is puckering up to enjoy a fantasy-filled night of kinky fun!

Star-Crossed Lovers Kiss

. . . .

The scene begins in one of your favorite cafés or bars. You stumble across an ex-lover (your present partner). It was one of the greatest love affairs of your life, but doomed from the start. Relive for this one evening, the passion and the fire you once shared. You have one night to ignite your old flames. From the moment of body contact, each kiss should be ecstasy, leading to ultimate surrender. Crazy love calls for the most torrid kisses!

. . . .

Tarzan and Jane Kiss

You're the king of her jungle. She's the love of your life. That is one mighty combination. This kiss is perfect for all the nature lovers. Plan a trek into the jungle with your sweetheart. Explore the terrain, the different animals, and listen to the sounds and smells of nature. Take your Jane in your arms and give her a long kiss that lets her know that she's your woman and you're her man.

Harlequin Kiss

Romance. Seduction. Fantasy. Mystery. Hot sex. These are all elements that make a great Harlequin romance. Enjoy a romantic evening of romance. Take time to seduce your partner through taste, smell, touch, sight, and hearing. Heighten your senses with rhythms of music, enticing aromas of food, the alluring smell and contact of freshly scented skin, and textures such as silk and velvet that add spark to your sexual drive. As your desire starts to peak, your kisses should also progress. The first kiss should be sweet and romantic, ending with a last kiss that will have you ripping each other's clothes off.

Sex in the City Kiss

Which one of the girls are you? Carrie Bradshaw, the fashionista writer, in search of can't-live-without-each-other love, who's stuck on her Mr. Big. Charlotte York, the eternal optimist and believer in love and finding your soul mate. Miranda Hobbes, the pessimistic, hard-hitting working girl who is softened by love. Or Samantha Jones, the successful sexy businesswoman and "try-sexual" who will try and do it all for the sake of good, hot sex. Whoever you are, kiss your man in the spirit of your chosen character. If you really want to spice things up, be all the women at once. He'll think he's kissing four different women!

• Fantasy Island Kiss •

Time for a vacation getaway. Pack your bags and get on a plane to a remote island: the Caribbean, South America, Southeast Asia, the Mediterranean—wherever you please . . . the world is your oyster. Spend passion-filled days and nights together far away from your routines and everyday lives. Live all your fantasies, explore every inch of each other's bodies, and discover endless buccal pleasures. On fantasy island, fantasies do come true.

Arabian Nights Kiss

Morocco is a perfect romantic destination for couples who want to deepen their spiritual connection. Cities like Casablanca, Fez, and Marrakech are synonymous with love and can transport you to another time and place. Your bedroom can be a perfect Arabian backdrop for reconnecting and spicy intimacy. Scent your room with incense and decorate it with floor pillows and cushions, candles, lanterns, canopy, drapes, etc. Use colors such as deep red and rich purple. Perfume your breath with common Moroccan spices like ginger or cinnamon. Spin a web of kisses for your partner in your Arabian harem that will have you both flying high on your magic carpet.

People with More Than Just Pucker

~ Mae West Kiss ~

"It's not the men in my life that counts, but the life in my men." The ballsy, free-spirited Mae West was known for these sultry double entendres. She was fierce, sexual, and raw, and made no excuses for it. This is that kind of kiss, one that is unapologetic and bold, sweeping you off your feet. From the moment your partner's lips touch yours, sparks ricochet off your skin and passions ignite. Your mouths are hungry for each other and your kisses unabashedly show it. As Mae West said, "It's not what I do, but the way I do it."

─── Betty Boop Kiss ───

Deliciously curvy, overtly sexual, and simply irresistible, Betty Boop embodied femininity. She could sashay across a room with her killer hips, leaving your imagination to its wiles. In her tight fitted dresses or racy corsets, her sexy garter belt, and high heels, her sex appeal was red hot. This kiss oozes sex. Greet your man wearing a fetching outfit that personifies a Betty Boop type of woman. Make sure he gets a good look at you. Work those feminine charms, girl! When you go in for the kiss, slurp him up. After this kiss, your man will know it's time to get down and dirty.

Rita Hayworth Kiss

La femme fatale Rita Hayworth was one of America's sexiest leading ladies. With a look, she could charm, with a flip of the hair, she could captivate. Her feminine charms held every man prisoner. This kiss makes your man prisoner to your love. It seduces him every time and makes him weak and purr like a kitty. In the movement of your lips and tongue, he can taste your desire, and it's burning hot! Keep the kisses coming, not letting up, until he surrenders completely to you.

• Marilyn Monroe Kiss •

She was referred to as the blond bombshell. Sultry. Vixen. Curvaceous. Vulnerable. A candle in the wind. She was desired by men and envied by women. Her beauty was in her complexity. This kiss shows every emotion in your heart. It starts out soft, and then progresses into a frenzy of kisses. It surprises, arouses, and impassions, and each one is unpredictable.

· *Carmen Kiss* ·

She's fiery hot. Her walk is like a dance. Her aura is spellbinding. Her kisses are addictive. No man could escape Carmen's seduction. It trapped men in her lover's net. A taste of your lady's lips will have him hooked on your love. Put on a flaming red dress and place a red flower in your hair. As soon as your man lays eyes on you, you have him in the palm of your hand. With your seductive manners, draw him to your lips. After you first kiss, suck and lick his entire body, marking him with your love.

Black Magic Woman Kiss

A man can't leave his black magic woman alone. She's put a spell on him with her tricks, licks, and lips. He keeps coming back for more, addicted as he is to her loving. Each time she kisses him, she entrances him. He loses himself in the heat of her lips. Each kiss is naughty and takes possession of him. After a night of her kisses, he'll be slave to her passion.

• Jezebel Kiss •

This kiss is bold and has no inhibitions. After this kiss, you will know what's on Jezebel's mind. She wants her man and this kiss tells him what she wants, how she wants it, and that she wants it now. Kiss the part of your man's body that turns you on the most. As you kiss him, drive him crazy with your lip action, insisting with deep strokes of your tongue. A Jezebel is merciless.

• Harlot Kiss •

You desire her and have to have her. You can't contain it any longer and you reach for your sweetheart. She pulls away and plays coy. She wants you to pay up. Big time! The price is the most valuable kisses in your repertoire. She wants those kisses that will send electric shocks throughout her body and set her on fire. She's not cheap either. She yearns for that lip and tongue action that breaks the bank. Do you have the resources to make her body heaven bound?

• Scarlett Kiss •

Red represents the color of love, passion, lust, power, and ecstasy. It's the flame of our innermost desires. It attracts our eye and arouses our libidos. Buy a pair of red sheets and put them on the bed. Dim the lights and lay your lover's naked body on the bed. Just the sight of the outline and curves of their body against a rich, sensuous red should be a quick turn on. Starting at their feet, kiss and give love bites to random parts until both your lips meet. By the time there's mouth-to-mouth contact, you'll be ready to get it on!

· Lady Chatterley's Kiss ·

This kiss unleashes the passion and sensual desire in your man. It's the kind of kiss that you have to start and finish. Turn off all the lights and sounds in your house and bedroom. Close your eyes so you're in utter darkness. This kiss relies on touch, taste, and smell. It begins with the contact of two bodies groping and exploring the carnal landscape and continues with hungry mouths feeding on each other. Hot, hot, HOT! This kiss will make your man ravenous for your love.

Lost in a Fairytale

· Cinderella Kiss ·

Prepare a special night out on the town with your lady. A cozy dinner for two in a dimly lit restaurant, a nightcap at a small jazz joint, the blues drifting in the background, and a stroll under a beam of moonlight. Up until this point, the intimacy between you has grown, but you have not kissed. At the stroke of midnight, take your sweetheart in your arms and give her a warmhearted kiss. No need for tricks here. This is just a full lip-on-lip kiss that says, "I love you."

• *Sleeping Beauty Kiss* •

Even while your sweetie sleeps, you desire her. You stare longingly at her, touching her face and lips. You bend down to hear her breathing. You want more and your lips part. You kiss her lips. Just one kiss, but it's enough to awaken her. You suck on her lips, teasingly, coaxing her from sleep. She begins to stir and slowly opens her eyes. You bend down and kiss her again. This time, you take her in your arms and make slow love to her.

Beauty and the Beast Kiss

This kiss tames the beast inside. It soothes and reassures. It feels like a sweet cup of hot chocolate or chicken soup for the soul. Is your partner having a bad day? Are they angry? Upset? Sad? Pet your partner's hair and run your hands through their hair. Focus on their eyes, their nose, their lips. Make them feel loved as your eyes drag across their face. Move your hand to the back of their neck and pull their face close to yours. Look into their eyes for a while and then focus on their lips. Slowly take their lips and tongue into yours. Now that should turn any beast into a kitty.

Popeye and Olive Oyl Kiss

Your love is one that has endured and weathered life's storms. It's solid and un-wavering. It's forever. This kiss expresses that kind of love. It celebrates your love each time your lips meet. Call it your special kiss. Stand together face to face. Just before you kiss, whisper, "I love you." Part your lips and feel the tap of your breaths. Open your mouths and take each other's tongue in. Make sure you get a good reserve of air because this kiss is a long one!

Kermit and Ms. Piggy Kiss

Your crush is HUGE. Your partner gives you butterflies. Your heart beats uncontrollably when you're in his presence. A simple touch of his hand send ripples of sensation throughout your body and makes your knees buckle. When your lips meet, you can hardly breathe. Your emotions swirl and your desire makes you dizzy. You're anxious and impatient and can't take it anymore. You grab his face and smother it in kisses. Even if your lover started this kiss, you're the one who finishes it.

Lady and the Tramp Kiss

Who can forget the unforgettable Italian dinner scene between the cocker spaniel, Lady, and the stray male mutt, Tramp. He was the bad boy from the other side of the tracks and she was the rich girl from a different world. Their attraction was palpable. Prepare a spaghetti dinner for your partner. Set one plate down at the table and sit side by side. Feed spaghetti to your partner. Slip the remaining spaghetti hanging from his mouth into yours, ingesting it until your lips touch. After you swallow the spaghetti, lick each other's lips and chins. Eating spaghetti was never sexier.

Romeo and Juliet Kiss

Your passion for each other is unabated. Each time you're in each other's arms, your bodies cling together as if inseparable. Your love is like a flame that never burns. This kiss is madly passionate. You fall into each other's arms, craving for love. Your lips lock immediately, your tongues greedily explore the inner sanctuaries of each other's mouths, and your hands grope hurriedly along each other's bodies. Your love is burning, so overwhelming that you topple to the floor, your mouths never parting.

I Love Jeannie Kiss

You're in the mood to grant your partner's every wish with a kiss. He wants kisses that sweeten, entice, tingle, burn, and drive him wild. Full lip and tongue action is what is needed here: varying tempo of your tongue, pressure of your lips, and slinking hands that double the pleasure. By the end of your lip-locking session, the master will want to grant your every wish!

Fairy Kiss

This is a secret kiss, given in the dead of night while your partner sleeps. This kiss is soft like a feather, almost imperceptible. When you lean over and plant your kiss, your lips barely touch your partner's. They'll never know that they were smooched.

Ken and Barbie Kiss

You both look fashionable tonight for a special night out on the town. He's decked out in a fetching suit, freshly scented, and looking quite dapper. You're a bombshell in your black cocktail dress, sexy pumps, and red-hot lipstick. You're both irresistible and wear a glow from all the day's lovemaking. Before you head out the door, give each other a passionate kiss, one that you have every intention of continuing once you're back home.

Chapter Five:
A Potpourri of Kisses

Kisses for Every Flavor of Love

Say It with a Kiss

• Diamond and Pearl Kiss •

You have a special gift for your sweetheart. You undress her and surprise her with diamonds or pearls, adorning her body with them. She looks like a queen. You can't take your eyes off her—the even tone of her skin, the scent of her body, the curve of her hips, the swell of her breasts. You've never desired her more than in this moment. You want to consume her, but savor her first. Your lips press firmly in her supple flesh. You inhale deeply. Your mouth opens slightly, you suck and bite softly. You relish her entire body before you feast on her lips.

· Insatiable Kiss ·

There are people who have a certain effect on you. They bring out the primitive in you, your rawest desires. Their presence raises your body temperature. Their touch causes your heart to pulse. Their kiss makes you scream and holler. You're insatiable when it comes to their loving.

This kiss is down and dirty. It's fearless and knows no bounds. From the moment your lips touch, hungry mouths set out on a carnal exploration that ends in fireworks.

Amore Kiss

You're walking on air, in a haze of euphoria. A rush of hormones have you feeling dizzy and drunk on love. Every time you see your sweetheart, it's like the first time. This kiss says loud and clear, "I LOVE you!" When you see your partner, dive in for the kiss. Grab the back of their head or the sides of their face and plant a hot wet one on their lips. That's amore.

• Bubbly Kiss •

When you're ready to go to bed, surprise your partner with a chilled bottle of champagne. Have fun with it. Toast to a night of hot fun. Let some trickle in each other's mouths and the rush of effervescence tingle your tongues. This kiss will taste so good. Drink and lick off each other's bodies. If you want to spice things up, wet your partner's gems with some bubbly and suck on the sweetness. Ooh la la . . .

• Cupid Kiss •

Sometimes, every couple needs a cupid kiss to inspire more romance in a love that's grown routine. This kiss inspires love, awakens passions, and makes your temperature rise. It's the kind of kiss that gets things rolling. It's very tactile. Before the kiss, there's the touch. You can't keep your hands off your partner. Be aware of their presence and keep touching them every chance you get. This sets the tone for the kiss. When your lips finally meet, give them one that's well worth it. After that kiss, they'll be smitten for good.

· Out of the Doghouse Kiss ·

Forgot to take out the trash? Forgot a birthday? Worse, your anniversary? You called your partner your ex's name?! Whatever the charge may be, this kiss will bail you out of the doghouse. This kiss is meaningful, yet tender. It starts out soft like a dab of cotton. A simple kiss on the lips, then another and another. Now, your lips part and you feel the tip of your partner's tongue, and then the slide and twist of your tongues. After that smooch, all will be forgiven.

· Sailor Kiss ·

You've been missing your sweetheart and can't wait to see them again. They've been away and your love has been through some terrible withdrawals. This kiss will give you the fix that you need. Like the love-crazed addict that you are, you run into their arms as soon you see your baby in the distance. Your lips press madly against each other's and you don't come up for air until you can't breathe anymore. That kiss should dock your lover's ship for a while!

• *Bliss Kiss* •

Love makes the sun shine on a rainy day. It makes all your worries melt away. It feels like a million dollars. Love is pure unadulterated bliss, and this kiss is, too. Close your eyes and pucker up. Get swept into each other's breath, lips, tongue. Dreamy. Floating. Divine.

• *Pandora's Box Kiss* •

This is not the kind of kiss you start and don't finish. When you take your sweet-heart in your arms, you have every intention of going all the way. This kiss drives your partner's libido through the roof. All parts are at work for this kiss to open Pandora's box—lips, tongue, teeth, hands, hips, mid section. Once your lips un-lock, your honey's floodgates will burst open.

Baby-making Kiss

• • •

Put on some smoky Barry White or velvety Luther Vandross, because this kiss is for the baby making kind of loving. It's for marathon love, all-night loving that makes you woozy, passionate, and downright lecherous. This kiss is all about sucking, licking, and biting. No holds barred. You're going all the way, consuming every bit of your lover. This kiss makes a woman feel fertile and a man feel virile. It serves up a big dose of sexual healing. Smoking hot!

Celebrate Love

~ Valentine Kiss ~

You are your sweetheart's Valentine every day of the year. This kiss is like a dozen roses, a box of chocolates, or a simple card. It expresses your love in an extra-special way. Surprise your partner with an affectionate kiss. Caress the parts of your partner's face that make them unique to you–their soft cheeks, pulpy lips, button nose, bouncy curls, or sleek locks. Then go in for the kiss and give your partner a warm, tender smooch that pulls at the heartstrings. When your lips part, keep your faces together and whisper sweet nothings.

Mistletoe Kiss

Who says you should toss out the mistletoe with the Christmas tree? Considered to have many magical attributes, you should definitely keep this green shrub year-round. Called an aphrodisiac, a bestower of fertility, and a ward against evil, the mistletoe calls for the ultimate smooch. For a kiss anytime of the year, hang the mistletoe above your partner's head, close your eyes, and pucker up! This kiss is more than just a peck. Let your partner taste your mouth—the hungry pull of luscious lips and the swirl of your juicy tongue.

Diamonds Are Forever Kiss

. . . .

Diamonds adorn and grace, tease and please, sparkle and luster. Like beautiful diamonds, a great kiss caresses her skin and lingers forever in your lady's mind. Cover your sweetheart's diamond wearing parts with your special kisses. Suckle on her earlobe and feed on her fingers. Kiss and lick around her neck, making her feel like she's wearing every stroke of your tongue. Every kiss will be worth millions.

. . . .

Just Hitched Kiss

You hear, "I now pronounce you husband and wife. You may kiss your bride." You better not give you new bride a skimpy kiss. This is the beginning of an entire life together. It warrants more than just a peck. Who cares if you have an entire congregation of folks watching?

Give each other a big portion of lip and tongue that you'll remember until death do you part. That means tongues thrusting and rolling, bodies wrapped up in each other's arms, and a lip-lock worthy of "I do."

Paper Kiss

It's been a year and you're still on the honeymoon. Still "lovey dovey," canoodling, and smooching every chance you get. Your lovefest has no plans of ending. Your partner's kiss still gives you butterflies in your stomach and sends tingles down your spine. When they plant one on you, your heart beats faster, your lips part and latch onto theirs, and your greedy tongue quenches its thirst. Your love is still burning and the fire is hot!

Anniversary Kiss

It's another year, and you're still together, loving and staying committed. If the flames of passion have cooled, this is a great time to reignite them. When you wake up in each other's arms, celebrate your anniversary with a kiss that begs for more. As soon as your sweetheart opens their eyes, lean over with a kiss that impassions the loins. This kiss starts out simple and builds as your desire lets loose. You stare into your partner's eyes, caress their face, finger their lips, slowly kiss, suck on their lips, the top one, and then the bottom one, until you finally surrender your entire mouth.

Tin Kiss

Ten years you've been with your baby and your love is still here to stay. That's a milestone that deserves a proper smooch. Make this a special anniversary night filled with kisses and hot loving. Create your own special kiss to celebrate a decade of deeper love and commitment. You've had lots of inspiration up until this point. Let those lips express all the fire in your heart. Make it romantic, kinky, sensual, erotic, or all of the above. Whatever you do, make sure you put ten years' worth of love into it.

Silver Kiss

Your love has endured a quarter of a century. Get out the bells and whistles; this kiss represents twenty-five years of the life you've built together. This kiss is strong and conquers your mind, body, and soul. Whether you renew your vows, take a special trip together, or lock yourselves in the bedroom for the night, this kiss is the cherry on top. Give your partner twenty-five different kisses, professing your love for each other in twenty-five different ways. From tender to raw, you'll cover the entire emotional spectrum of your love. Heavenly!

Gold Kiss

Your love has kept you together for half a century. Any love that has that kind of staying power deserves an extraordinary kiss. This kiss is celestial and feels like two souls touching. Put on one of your favorite golden oldies. Dance in each other's arms, kissing to the rhythm of love until the end of the song. When your lips press together, you feel one with your partner. The sensations travel deep within you. This kiss is slow and tender, not involving any special tricks. Give your partner kiss after kiss after kiss. Keep them coming. Like your love, this kiss lasts forever.

Diamond Kiss

Originating from ancient Greece, the word "diamond" means unbreakable. After sixty years of dedication and love, a diamond kiss is most fitting. Your love has lasted a lifetime. You're two love warriors who have braved life's ups and downs, and your love is triumphant! The kiss is one of soulmates. Give your partner a simple kiss on the lips. Then spend the entire night wrapped up in each other's arms, nestled by the love of two old souls.

Just the Two of Us

Chéri(e) Kiss

This kiss is for the dear and special one, your significant other who you endearingly call your sweetheart, darling, honey, baby, or chéri(e). It's sweet and affectionate and stakes its claim on you. This kiss is given anytime during the day—whenever the love bug bites. Find a place where your partner can feel the warmth of your love. Kiss your love's neck, shoulder, lips, forehead, or hand. Then take them in your arms and squeeze tight!

• *Sweetie Pie Kiss* •

This kiss is for your one and only, the one who takes your breath away. You take one look at them and you feel this incredible urge to just plant one on them. You lean over and take their face in your hands and kiss them squarely on the lips. Bam! End your smooch on the lips with a snuggle of your nose. Take the opportunity to whisper something sweet, romantic, or naughty!

• Teddy Bear Kiss •

Curl up next to your lover. It's the coziest place to be. Their body is a magnet and draws you near. You can't resist being blanketed in their warmth. Press your bodies together, wrap your arms around each other, and slowly kiss and suck on each other's lips. Your partner's lips feel plush, their arms soft around you, and their body loveable. Hmm, that's one teddy bear you'll want to sleep with every night!

• Canoodle Kiss •

An afternoon of fondling, anyone? Take a lazy afternoon and put it to good use. Before you get to your lover's lips, give some TLC to their body. A heavy session of petting will get their lips wet and puckered. Caress their entire body from head to toe. When you're done, suckle on your partner's lips and tongue and continue down to their neck, alternating with your magic touch. Now it's your turn to get the same TLC that you served up.

• *Sunrise Kiss* •

The sun is inching over the horizon, peeking through your bedroom window. You're nestled in each other's warmth, your arms and legs entangled. You slowly open your eyes and the first rays of the sun hit your face. Your partner begins to stir and you squeeze them harder in your arms. You give them light kisses on the forehead, nose, and cheeks. When you get to their lips, you turn up the heat. You apply more pressure and your kisses become long and deliberate. Your partner can't resist and begins to respond. You sink further under the sheets and set your bed on fire.

After Midnight Kiss

It's the dead of the night. You've tried counting sheep. You're tired of staring at the ceiling, tossing and turning in bed. You've got one thing on your mind, and that's L-O-V-E. Your partner sleeps soundly next to you, but you can't keep your hands to yourself. Slip your hands under their pajama top to feel the smooth glide of their skin. You're revved up and inch closer. Kiss your partner's outer ear, and then suck on their earlobe. Slowly wake up your partner with dirty talk and naughty whispers that will preheat the oven for some hot loving.

• *Smooch Kiss* •

When was the last time you both had a hot and heavy make-out session? During your honeymoon? When you were courting each other? Time to add smooching back to your sexual menu. Grab your partner in a lip-lock in the bedroom, shower, on the couch, while they're cooking dinner. Knock them off their feet with lip and tongue action that feels like fireworks. All parts are at work—lips, tongue, sucking, licking, and biting. If this kiss is done right, when your lips part, both of you should feel dizzy!

• Spooning Kiss •

This kiss creates a moment of intense connection with your partner. Facing the same direction on your sides, lay your back to your partner's chest. Like two spoons against each other, it's a perfect fit. This kiss is much more pleasurable when both of you are naked. Feel the heat of each other's skin, your partner's breath on your back, the tickle of their fingers along your side. Your desire is climbing. Feel your partner's hips get even closer to you, their wet lips kissing your back firmly, their fingers grazing your nipples. When you start moaning and groaning, turn around to put yourself out of your misery!

• Fireplace Kiss •

The fireplace is blazing. The fire is crackling. You're snuggling in each other's arms on a cold winter's night. The heat from the fire and from your lover's body is making your desire climb sky-high. The moment is intensely erotic. You can't let you go of your partner's body and your lips never part. This kiss goes on forever, sucking and tasting each other's mouths. It's passionate from the first kiss until the last.

Weekend Kiss

It's the end of a long, busy week and you're ready to get your weekend started. Time to reconnect with your partner. When you sleep in Saturday morning, take time for some pillow talk and a lip-smacking session that will start the weekend off in a romantic state of mind. Show lip love to different parts of your partner's body. Let them feel every bit of your desire from the rapturous kiss and pull of your lips. This could be the incentive to spend an entire weekend in bed!

Picnic Kiss

Prepare a picnic basket and take the afternoon off with your sweetheart. Head to your local park and spread out a blanket. Kick off your shoes and start your feast. After you've done toasting and dining, it's time to serve up a bunch of smooches. With the smell of fresh grass all around you and the sun beaming above, linger in each other's arms. Share tender, sweet kisses, basking in romance. Bliss never felt that good!

Seasonal Kisses

• Autumn Kiss •

The warmth of summer gives way to the briskness of autumn. Days get shorter, skies become grayer, and leaves fall from the trees. As temperatures decrease, this kiss will warm you up for the chill of winter. As you begin to hibernate more indoors, take the time to cuddle with your significant other and make out. You have a repertoire of kisses at your disposal, which will keep you snug throughout the winter season.

• *Autumn Leaves Kiss* •

The palette of autumn color is majestic—nature's way of seducing us before her winter hibernation. A kaleidoscope of color ranging from orange, yellow, red, and brown paints the landscape before falling to the ground. Take long walks with your partner and when you start to feel the bite of autumn's crisp air, warm up with a kiss that will make you both blush. Wrapped in the arms of your lover against a backdrop of color, give each other a long kiss to turn up your bodies' temperature.

Wintergreen Kiss

Even during winter, some of mother nature's offspring continue to flourish. Don't let your libido hibernate until the first days of spring. Melt the frost of winter with sizzling kisses. As your lover steps in from the cold, warm up their lips with your hot smooch. Slightly part your lips and place your mouth on theirs, kissing them until their lips are not the only parts heating up!

Season of Love Kiss

It's springtime and love is in blossom. Passions awaken, flowers flourish, and the rains wash the winter drear away. There's pep in your step and a spark in your kiss. When you grab your lover in your arms, your kiss lets them know that your desire has not been dormant. Your tongue is fast and furious and slides completely into your lover's mouth. Hold them tight! Your sexual appetite will devour them.

April in Paris Kiss

The city of love during spring will charm lovers and revive passions. Paris is irresistible. A long stroll through the enchanting Parisian streets as the sun sets over the Seine River. Café terraces paired with lovers locked in embraces. Park benches nestled in graveled historic parks. The wind of cobblestone streets, the bloom of fragrant flowers, and a magnificent landscape of art and architecture. Every part of Paris is made for a kiss. Pick any spot in this bewitching city and sweep your lover away with a languorous kiss. You'll be kissing all over the city.

Spring Fever Kiss

The hot days of summer are fast approaching. The temperature rises every day along with your excitement. Spring is well underway and you're restless for some sizzle. A dog in heat when you see your lover, you can't control yourself and pull them into your arms. Your lips smash together in an intense embrace. Pull your lover to the floor and kiss every stitch of their skin. Be merciless and make their body burn with your lip action.

Summer Solstice Kiss

It's the end of June and summer is here. Take a walk on the beach, around town, or in the city with that special person in your life. This kiss is easy and breezy, light like the summer wind. As the sun starts to set, stand still or sit down, pulling your partner's back against your chest. Caress their hair and kiss their neck while they watch the sun disappearing behind the horizon. Pull their head to yours and express your feelings with a simple kiss. This kiss is the perfect dose of perfection as you bask in the rays of your love.

Sizzle Kiss

It's one of the hottest days of the summer. It's sweltering and it feels like you're walking through a furnace. When you get home, strip off your clothes and pull your sweetheart into a cool shower with you. Cup your hands to gather water in your palms and pour it over parts of your partner's body. The splash of the water feels refreshing. Now finger the most erogenous zones of their body with one hand while you let them suck on a finger on your other hand. As you drive them wild, push them against the cold tile for a kiss that will have them gasping for air!

Passion Fest

• Adam and Eve Kiss •

Begin your night of passion by taking off your clothes while your partner watches. No touching or kissing the forbidden fruit yet. Now it's their turn. Let your eyes peruse the goods. Now that both of you are standing in the buck, let the fireworks begin. Take your beloved in your arms and give them a simple kiss on the lips. No mouth gymnastics here. Just soft kisses. Innocent. Loving. Enticing. Don't stop. Keep them coming one after the other. The feel of their skin and the increased pressure of your lips should heighten some of your senses. Feel the desire building and when you can't take it anymore, unleash the passion.

• *Mirror Kiss* •

When was the last time you really stared down your partner? The last time you really looked deeply into someone's eyes and let what you saw speak for itself. Well, this is the kiss that allows you to see into your beloved's heart. Face your partner, mirroring each other. Remain close. Very close. Intertwine your fingers. Let your eyes speak the truths of your heart. Shh!! No words. No whispers. Just let the sound of your breath fill the space between you. Lean in close and plant a kiss on your partner's lips. Your lover should do the same. Take turns giving one kiss. After each embrace, keep gazing into each other's eyes. Kiss. Gaze. Kiss. Gaze. Magnetic! Let your eyes mirror the love and let the sparks fly.

• Holy Kiss! •

This kiss is one of the most sensual. You can do it in a variety of positions and never tire of the sensations it gives you. Take your partner's face in both hands. Start a trail of kisses down their face, the forehead being the starting point. Slightly part your lips as you descend to taste their skin. Continue down between their eyes, the tip of the nose, each lip, the chin, and the neck. Start another trail of kisses across their face. From left to right, kissing the ear, cheek, tip of the nose, cheek, and other ear. Apply minimum pressure, only lightly pressing your lips against each part. Your lover will feel anointed by your tongue. To add a twist while giving this kiss, straddle your partner and rotate your hips at the same time. The feeling is just divine!

· Crimson Kiss ·

You've showered and your skin is silky smooth with the killer scent of a seductress. As you check the time, your man is due home any minute. For the finishing touches, put on red-hot lipstick. When your special man finally enters the bedroom, greet him on the bed wearing only your crimson colored lips. When he approaches, help him out of his clothes. When he's also wearing his birthday suit, leave lipstick-colored kisses all over his body. After you're done marking his body, give him a final kiss on his lips that will make your male cub turn into a lion!

Say My Name Kiss

While romping in the sack with your Romeo or Juliette, smother them in lip and tongue action that makes their body heaven bound. Make sure the lovemaking and the lip smacking are in sync. A steady rhythm is sure to reach orgasmic heights. When your partner is about to peak, adjust your position and suck on their nipples. Ooh! Ahh! They'll be screaming your name.

• Scarlet Letter Kiss •

In the mood for a raunchy night of sinful foreplay? Put your tongue skills to good use. Draw different letters on your lover's skin with your wet tongue. Lick and blow to heighten their senses. Stay in one area or cover different body parts that you find most enjoyable. When you're done, your partner should feel like they're wearing the sins of your tongue on them. Kisses like these should be forbidden!

Love Haze Kiss

After a passionate night of lovemaking with your body glistening with sweat, sheets soaked through, your body shivering from an explosion of emotions, and your vision blurred from crazy loving, end with a kiss that soothes the rage of your desire. Hold your partner's limp body in your arms and kiss them softly on the lips and face. When their breathing returns to normal and sleep begins to tug at their eyelids, whisper how much you love them before dozing off to sleep.

Strip Down Kiss

Take off your lover's clothes item by item, sucking on their exposed body parts. Take your time undressing your partner, playing up the seduction. When they are fully naked, place them on the bed. Work your way up from their feet to their lips and back down again. By the time you come back up to their lips, your partner will be ready to take things to the next level!

• Tickle Kiss •

Before you turn on the heat, enjoy some playful fun with your partner. What are the ticklish areas of your lover's body? Lightly brush your lips against those parts. Alternate with your tongue to add texture and blow on your saliva. These kisses will have your partner's body contorting and squirming in every direction, and when they beg for mercy, slip your tongue in their mouth for a swirl. Instead of mercy, they'll be begging for more.

• Zing Kiss •

Give your partner a kiss with a zest of something extra special. What kind of mood are you in? Romantic, loving, horny, passionate, or enamored? Whatever the feeling, say it with a kiss and add something that will drive your partner over the sexual edge. It could be sexual props, blindfolds, a spanking, whipped cream, ice cubes, etc. Double up your kiss with any of these things and set your bed ablaze. Oh my, if only the walls could talk!

Chapter Six:
Kisses for the Adventurous

Kisses That Make You Beg for More

A Splash of Kisses

Shower of Kisses

There's nothing more erotic than warm water falling over your body from your head to your toes, beating against your skin. Increase your pleasure and pull your partner into the shower with you. As the water rains down on you, passionately embrace your lover. Don't hold back! By now, you've learned a few techniques, so try a hot combination. Suck your lover's lips and tongue. French kiss. Mirror kiss. Lobe kiss. With nothing but the sound of water, the slip and slide of hands all over your body, and tongues intertwining, the temperature will be muy caliente!

Steamy Kiss

A cloud of hot steam fills your bathroom. Pearls of perspiration trickle down your back. A veil of sweat glistens on your bodies. Your lover's hand slips and slides down your moist skin. As the heat rises, your movements become elongated and sensual. The rising temperature lures out your passions and your sexual appetite is gaping wide open. You pet each other and kiss. Your lips are voracious for your partner's flesh. When you become inflamed with passion, pull your partner out of the bathroom and head for the boudoir!

Rubber Ducky Kiss

Dim the lights, light some soothing candles, fill two glasses with wine or champagne, and prepare a bubble bath. It's time for some sexy relaxation with your beloved. Have your partner sit between your legs with her back against you or sit facing each other, your legs intertwined. Soak up the bubble while you reconnect with your amour. This kiss involves an erotic combo of hands, feet, and lips. Fondle and massage your lover's body or pleasure each other with your extremities and mouth. Explore and discover many delights under the bubbles.

Wet and Slippery Kiss

It started out with a make-out session under the showerhead that would make even Cupid blush. While you devoured your lover's body, hot water gushed down over your bodies making you even more lustful for each other. When your passions start to sizzle, pull your lover out of the shower and lay them down, still dripping wet, on your bed. Slide on top of them. The feel of two slippery bodies meshing together in passion is an aphrodisiac in itself! Continue your lip-locking session that got you back in bed and, this time, take it all the way!

Suds of Kisses

Lather up each other's bodies when you and your honey are in the shower together, covering your entire bodies in soap. When your bodies are completely soapy, take your lover into your arms and give them a whopping kiss on the lips. Let your hands roam all over each other's bodies, gliding up and down your backs and over the hump of your butts. Turn them around and kiss them from behind while you caress their chest. Let the taste of your sweetheart's mouth and the sensation of the sensual slip of your hands inspire new fantasies.

Neptune Kiss

Swimming under water is one of the most pleasurable experiences to have with your lover. Whether you're in the ocean or in a swimming pool, water makes your body feel light and natural. As the water caresses your bodies, cling to each other and kiss. Share all types of kisses with your lover and let the sway of the water carry you. Take a dip under water and swim into each other's arm, kissing all the way to the surface. Feels magical!

Splish Splash Kiss

Looking to cool down from the sweltering heat in the summer? Enjoy an afternoon at your local park, splish splashing in the sprinklers. Take off your shoes and grab your partner's hands. Run through the refreshing spray of water or stay under it. Pull your partner into your arms and give them a big juicy kiss. As your wet clothes cling to your bodies and the water rains down on both of you, feel the excitement and passions bubbling. Instead of a cool down, you'll burn up!

Dolce Vita Kiss

Be adventurous. Be daring. Be sexy! Let your fantasies run wild. As the Italians say, it's la dolce vita, "the sweet life." Happiness makes you do crazy things sometimes. Take a dip in a public fountain. Kick off your shoes and splash in the fountain. Get your man to come inside with you. If he resists, lure him in with your sexy poses and your sexy begging. Once he gets in, take his face into your hand and look at him like a hungry cougar. Let him see how much you want and desire him. Caress his face and neck. Kiss him affectionately and then passionately!

Singing in the Rain Kiss

Rain has incredible energy. It's intensely electric and passionate. Caught in a downpour with the rain lashing your body, wrapped in your lover's arms, and locked in an embrace can be one of the most erotic feelings in the world. It heightens every emotion and makes your desire skyrocket. The next time it's raining, take the time to smooch with your sweetheart. Snuggle under an umbrella or without and lose yourselves in the heat of each other's mouths.

Skinny-dipping Kiss

• • •

Alone on a hot summer's night with your lover? Why don't you go for a swimming excursion. A pool, a lake, the beach, or even a Jacuzzi is perfect for your tryst in the water. Strip down and jump in. Play hanky panky in the water and under the stars with your partner. Let the sexual beast out of its cage and give your partner the boldest kisses. No one will know of your nightly exploits except the man in the moon.

Très Risqué

～ Butterfly Kiss ～

This kiss is perfect for a playful romp in the sand or grass or even on your bed. Place your partner on the bottom, and get on top. The bottom partner outstretches his arms and legs. Kiss him on the lips while his arms and legs flutter to the sides like the wings of a butterfly. Hold him by the sides while he moves and kiss him steadily. The slight resistance and movement of his body create a sexual friction that raises your sexual barometer!

Henna Kiss

Spend an afternoon decorating your lover's body in sexy art. Use anything that tickles your fancy—lipstick, whipped cream, honey, washable ink, fake tattoos, or henna. If your drawings are edible, suck and lick them off your partner. If it's ink, outline your art with your tongue before you paint it on their skin. Either way, the sensations are sinfully pleasurable.

Massage Kiss

Dim the lights, light soothing candles, and prep aromatic oils and lotions. Get ready for an erotic evening of massage. Massage your lover's body, kneading their flesh, lingering on their erogenous zones. Drive them wild with the tips of your fingers. When they're putty in your hands, scoop them up in your arms and give them a tonguing worthy of all the passion in your heart.

• Elevator Kiss •

The next time you're alone in the elevator with your sweetheart, box them in a corner and look deeply into their eyes. Caress their lips with your finger, outlining the shape. You can't wait until you get behind closed doors and begin to spin a passionate web to trap your lover. Slowly lean into them and kiss their lips. This kiss quickly progresses into full lip and tongue action. When the doors finally open, take your partner by the hand and whisper the naughty things you're going to do to them when you get home.

· Stairwell Kiss ·

Instead of getting on the elevator, take the stairs. Pin your sweetheart against the wall and steal some kisses. Since you have the stairwell to yourselves, let your hands roam to those private parts that are addicted to the feel of your fingers. Make this kiss a spicy one. Suck hard on each other's tongue while you enjoy arousing each other. Keep the moaning and groaning down if you don't want to get busted!

Voodoo Kiss

This kiss puts a spell on your lover and makes them addicted to your love. They've never been kissed like that—never even knew that lips and a tongue had such skill and precision. Create a signature kiss that drives your partner crazy. Each time you give them that kiss, it will reach down deep into their soul and possess them. Use every skill you've learned up until this point and make your lover a slave to your kiss.

∙ Groove Kiss ∙

Put on your favorite slow jam, pull your partner in your arms, and start grooving to a sexy melody. Your hips are grinding, your mid section is gyrating, and the love beast in you is roaring. As you bump and grind, kiss your partner and let your lips move to the rhythm of the beat. This creates an intimate, erotic moment and puts your lover immediately in the mood for a night of hot-blooded loving.

· Pacifier Kiss ·

Give your tongue a rest. This kiss only calls for the skill of your lips and teeth. Suck and lightly bite your lover's mouth. It should feel as if you're sucking on a sweet, soft, juicy pacifier. The pull and the suck of your lips give them tingles and heighten every sensation in their body. The feeling is euphoric if done correctly.

Slurpy Kiss

You're in the throes of passion. Your desire is unleashed, unabashed, and voracious. You're an animal. This is an orgy of lip, tongue, and teeth, sucking, licking, and biting your partner. Slurp up all of your partner's juices. Your mouth is busy at work consuming every part of your lover's body. Not one part of them will be left unexplored!

Pelvic Kiss

● ● ●

You're deep in foreplay and heading south on your lover's body. You stop between their bellybutton and pubic hair. Start pleasuring their bellybutton with your tongue, tickling it with the very tip. You're such a tease. Suck their flesh as your head further south, and then, with varying pressure, lick their pelvic area, unleashing a bevy of sensation, from ticklish to erotic. This kiss is O-R-G-A-S-M-I-C!

Wild Kingdom

~ Kitty Kiss ~

Since your baby has gotten home, you've been purring like a kitty. You're starving for some TLC. You approach and snuggle up against your lover's body on the couch. Rub your nose and lips against his neck. Caress his body and lift your partner's shirt up, nuzzling against his chest. Give him little kisses and light licks on his chest, arms, and hands. When you're done petting, rest your head on his lap and claim your space. Meow!

• Doggie Kiss •

One minute apart from your lover is unbearable. When he isn't in your presence, your heart aches and thoughts of him swirl in your mind. You've been restless for his love all day long, and when you hear him come through the door, you charge and jump in his arms. Smother his face, lips, and neck in kisses and licks. Your kisses are full of excitement and desire. Make sure you don't slobber all over him. Spit control is key in keeping your beloved turned on. So, mark your territory!

• Bambi Kiss •

When your man comes into the bedroom, greet him with seduction. With your doe eyes, you're an innocent Bambi. You're soft and delicate with your touch and inviting in your white lace bra and panties. Take off your man's clothes and lay him on the bed. Climb on top and start petting, kissing, and caressing him in places that unlock his innermost fantasies. There aren't any kinks or tricks here, just pure affection. Your delicate stroke and tender kiss will have your man mesmerized by your touch.

Cougar Kiss

The sexy feline is on the prowl. She has a big appetite and her man is her prey. She's in charge tonight and will pursue you until you surrender. When you enter her domain, she claws your clothes off and pins you to the floor. Her desire roars and she's ravenous. Each of her kisses sears the heat of her passion into your skin. She bites, sucks, licks, and practically consumes your entire mouth. When she releases you from her clenches, you'll be a mangled heap of bones.

King Kong Kiss

You've gone ape for your lady. You're nuts for her loving. She's been away all day and you've been restless in your cage. When she gets home, you snatch her up, throw her over your shoulder, and carry her to the bedroom. She loves the feeling of being enraptured by a wild beast. It turns her on and she gladly succumbs to your passion. By this time, she's hot and ready. Give her kisses that are forceful and remind her who's the most powerful beast in her jungle. After those kisses, you can rip off her clothes!

Gazelle Kiss

It's mating season and you have hot sex on your mind all the time. Just the sight and the smell of your mate turn you into a sex-crazed animal any time of the day. Right now, you want your man and you zone in for the kill. Your movements are graceful as you slink toward him on the floor. Your eyes are pooling with desire and your hunger for him. As you approach, you caress him gradually, unbutton his shirt, kissing his chest after each button pops open. By the time you reach his lips, your man will be your prisoner of love.

King of the Jungle Kiss

The King of the jungle has many facets. His beauty is majestic, his strength powerful. He's a fierce protector of his territory, yet he's bashful at times. This kiss is all of those things. Show your woman all the different sides of your love. Tender and sweet kisses. Aggressive and bold kisses. Fierce and passionate kisses. Alternate with touching, licking, head rubbing, licking, and purring. Show your darling that your roar is bigger than your bite.

Octopus Kiss

This kiss is all in the touch. While you're smooching on your lover's lips, your hands are caressing every part of them. Your hands are constantly moving and all your fingers should be strumming their most sensitive parts. Wrap your lover's body in your tentacles and get to work. Your touch should bring every sensation in your partner's body to life. It should feel like you have eight hands instead of two!

Snake Kiss

While your lover sleeps, slither under the covers. Feel them up to arouse them from sleep. Burrow under the covers until your reach their face. Use the flicker of your tongue on their stomach, chest, nipples, etc. to increase your partner's pleasure. Finally, constrict their hands and bite their neck. Your love venom will be deadly!

Fish Kiss

This kiss is one the sweetest ones to give. It's for any time of the day. Take your partner's face in your hands and pucker up. Give your sweetheart little kisses all over their face. This kiss is pure bliss, deep affection, and a heap of love. If love is in the kiss, you'll feel every bit of your honey's amour in this one.

Voyeurism

~ City of Kisses ~

Plan an entire day of outdoor fun around the city. It's been a long time since you've been to your favorite hangouts, parks, neighborhoods, cafés, clubs, museums, etc. While playing tourist, be romantic, intimate, flirtatious, and mischievous. Don't be shy just because you're in public. From morning to late at night, paint the town with your kisses.

Alley Cat Kiss

Duck into an empty alley with your sweetheart. You're both horny for each other's love and can't wait until you get home. So, you steal a moment away from passersby to kiss. Pin your lover against the side of a building. Pause before kissing. Look into their eyes. Lick your lips, then theirs. Look into their eyes again. Kiss them slowly, progressively working your way up to a full make-out session. This kiss is potent. Your head will spin and you'll feel like you're floating away.

Platform Kiss

Trains enter the station with a thunderous roar. The clangor of steel and metal rips through your ears. Strangers litter the platform, but you're in the arms of your significant other. In the midst of all the bustle, time stands still. You whisper sweet nothings into each other's ears and share tender kisses. These whispers and kisses will drown out all the sound and make everything around you invisible. You'll feel like the only two people in the world.

• Bus Kiss •

You're packed like sardines on a crowded bus. As the bus lurches forward, you wrap your arms around your partner's waist while they hold onto the railing. Press your body close to your partner's and feel their mid sections within a hair's breadth yours. The closeness of their body in a public place arouses you. Give your lover a big kiss on the lips. Give them another one. If you're bold enough, keep kissing until it's time to get off.

· Taxi Kiss ·

You hop into a taxi with your lover after a night on the town. The chemistry between you is electric. You lay your hand on your partner's thigh, but you're too hot and bothered to keep it there. Your hand travels up your lover's thigh. You eye the driver, and then get a little bolder. Grab your partner's face and kiss them. Ease down into the seat as your kisses get more intense. Without a care in the world, enjoy your lip-lock until the taximeter stops running.

• *Movie Kiss* •

Take your sweetheart to a matinee. Head to the last row, choosing the middle seats. The theater probably won't be too crowded. When the lights go out, start making out. Your entire head is moving, all parts of your mouth. This if full lip-on-lip action. Shh! Try to stifle your sounds of pleasure. By the time you come up for air, the movie will have finished!

• *Street Kiss* •

You're in the middle of the street and suddenly you stop and pull your lover into your arms. Your emotions are bubbling inside and you plant one big kiss on them. Oblivious to the people walking around you, you kiss for a long time, and then remain in each other's arms awhile before continuing on your way again. Ain't love swell!

· *Table Kiss* ·

Tonight, you're heading out to your favorite restaurant for a cozy dinner for two. When you arrive at the table, you decide to sit side by side instead of so far away facing each other. Order drinks and a three-course meal to follow. Feed your lover and kiss all the way to the dessert. By the time you finish, you'll feel the scorch of your passion. Check, please!

• Club Kiss •

When was the last time you let loose in a club? It's time for a night of dancing, for some booty shaking, hip grinding, and body grooving with you partner. Grab your partner and hit the dance floor. No inhibitions. No wallflowers. Get out there and do your thing. Let the music carry you and shake what you got. As you get into the rhythm, share some groovy kisses. Each song should inspire a different kind of kiss. Don't be shy and let out the dirty dancer in you.

Lawn Kiss

• • •

Spend an afternoon at the park or in your backyard with your significant other. Spread a blanket out and lie out in the sun, your bodies intertwined. As you chat the afternoon away, share sexy smooches. These kisses range from spicy to sweet. When you start to sizzle under the sun, take the smooch fest behind close doors.

X-Rated

~ Booty Call Kiss ~

You can't get your sweetheart out of your mind. Your thoughts are naughty ... downright indecent. Pick up the phone and call your lady or man. Tell them you have to see them immediately, that you have to caress their skin, taste their mouth, and feel their tongue and lips against yours. Your desire won't take no for answer. When the doorbell finally rings, answer in your birthday suit and pucker up.

• Hit and Run Kiss •

This kiss is quick, but thorough. You're on the run but always have time for a proper smooch with your baby. Put your juicy lips and luscious mouth to better use than for a stingy peck. Even on the go, you can take your honey in your arms and give them a kiss that lasts more than a sec. Take time to fully feel their lips on yours, slightly part your mouth to smell and feel their breath, taste their tongue, twist it around theirs. Now that's worth your time!

• *Ravenous Kiss* •

You're hungry for your sweetheart's loving and can no longer contain your desire. As soon as you get them in your arms, sweep them off your feet with a passionate kiss. Your lips smash together, you tongues move in a swirl of frenzy, and your hands caress each other in crazed excitement.

Fetish Kiss

. . . .

What's your delight? Toes? Tongues? Nipples? Earlobes? Whips or Handcuffs?
Whipped cream or honey? Whatever it is, create a kiss that sets the tone for your
favorite kinky play. You have an entire repertoire at your disposal to inspire your
cravings. Let your imagination run wild!

. . . .

Telephone Kiss

You're away from your lover and miss their kiss—the feel of their lips and tongue, the taste of their mouth, and the smell of their breath. Call their number for a phone kiss. Let them describe their favorite kiss or how they'll kiss you the next time they see you. Then it's your turn. Be graphic and share all the sexy details. That should hold you over until you get the real thing!

Backseat Kiss

The next time you're in the car with your significant other, turn off the gas, park in a quiet area, and hop in the back seat. Take some time out to smooch and fog up the windows with your passion. There's something wildly erotic about clawing at your man or woman in the backseat of the car and tonguing them down out where anyone could walk by. It adds fire to the excitement and drives your libido off the Richter scale!

Boudoir Kiss

Lock your bedroom doors and get ready for a trip to the wild side. Prepare your love chamber with candles, fragrant scents, rose petals, champagne, strawberries, dimmed lights, sexy lingerie, etc. Each of his senses should be pleasured. Nonstop pleasure of all the senses will bring his desire to the brink. When you lover can't take anymore, send him over the edge.

Cyber Kiss

Missing your baby? Don't fret; love is just a mouse click away. Get out the web cam and start a cyber chat with your significant other. Long gone are the days when you have to wait weeks or months before seeing your man or lady again. Get a sneak preview with a private cyber chat. Blow kisses, show your baby where you want to be kissed, or get real close to the cam and pucker up.

Upside Down Kiss

This kiss is rated XXX. It's for those lovers who aren't afraid to explore ALL the boundaries. Lie down with your partner facing the opposite direction. You can start this kiss on top of each other or on your sides, gradually adjusting your position as you make your way up your lover's body. Start at the feet, and then go where desire dictates. Get more risqué as you get higher. By the time you both reach each other's lips, your desire will be smoking!

Tattoo Kiss

Mark your lover's body with love bites. Suck their skin, leaving your marks of passion. This kiss calls for a slow suck for the red hickey to show up on the skin. It feels like a sting, one that is most pleasurable and satisfying. There's no rushing a kiss like this.

Chapter Seven:
The Virtuoso Kisser

Kisses of a Kama Seducer

Parlez-Vous Français?

Basic French Kiss

If you haven't mastered this kiss, you've never really given a kiss. This kiss is one of the first intimate experiences you'll share with your lover and it takes things to another level. Tilt your head slightly and look into your partner's eyes as your faces approach. When your lips touch, close your eyes. Part your lips and slowly slide your tongue into your partner's mouth. This is playtime for your tongues. Let your tongues roll and twist or brush and slide against each other. Make sure you're both following the same rhythm. Even pacing feels so good. Don't forget to breathe to keep going as long as your tongues desire!

— French Kiss with a Twist —

Now that you've become quite adept at the art of the French kiss, it's time to add a twist. Combine the French kiss with any one of your favorite kisses. They're so many to choose from. Alternate between both kisses until both of you are intoxicated with passion.

French Kiss Sans Lips

This kiss is made especially for your tongues. Lick each other's tongues, twist them around, and suck on the tips. Saliva control is very important for this kiss. No one likes to kiss a wet, sopping tongue. Done right, this kiss raises your libido. Feel the friction and enjoy the growing sensation of your tongue exploration.

Bisous à la Mode Kiss

This kiss is sweet as can be. Spread whipped cream, vanilla ice cream, honey, or your favorite sugar delight on your lips. Ask your partner to lick it off or kiss each other to share. You'll satisfy both your libido and sweet tooth.

• Bon Appétit Kiss •

You've planned a smoking hot dinner. The main course—your lover! Spread them on the table, take their clothes off, and feast on their sexy parts for dinner. Kiss, suck, and bite until you've gotten your full. Absolutely succulent.

· Bonjour Kiss ·

As your sweetheart's eyes slowly open in the morning, the first thing they see is your face, waiting to shower them with kisses. You lick your lips, slightly open your mouth, and lean down. They close their eyes and pucker up, waiting to be swept up in the sweetest embrace.

• Au Revoir Kiss •

Give your lover a goodbye kiss they'll never forget. Full lip and tongue action is required. At the end of this kiss, let your lips cling to your partner's. Linger in the heat of each other's mouths. That should keep you both warm until the next kiss!

• *Rendezvous Kiss* •

Give your lover a time and place to meet. It could be your favorite restaurant, café, hangout, park, or street corner. Once you meet, fall into each other's arms and kiss. Just kiss and kiss like you're the only two people in the world.

· *Apéritif Kiss* ·

After work, put on some of your favorite tunes and prepare a signature cocktail for you and your lover. A twist of lime, two ounces of spicy rum, and lots of kisses. Share simple kisses as well as long make-out smooches. This is a great kiss for reconnecting after a hectic day. Evening cocktails and kisses are a perfect transition into a night of love.

Toilette Kiss

When your lady steps out the shower, greet her with a towel. Slowly pat her dry like she's a queen. Next, massage her entire body with her favorite lotion, giving all her sexy parts major TLC. When you're done, instead of spraying her with her favorite perfume, give her kisses on her neck, wrists, and in between her breasts. She'll be wearing (and recalling) them all day long.

Props 'n' Things

— Chair Kiss —

Tell your sexy man to shed his clothes and take a seat. Now it's his turn for a sexy striptease. When you're completely naked, sit on your man and give him a sexy lap dance. Work those hips and butt to get things heated up. When the chair starts to shake, grab his face and give him a tonguing down that will make you both go up in flames!

Pole Kiss

Show your man the naughty things a pole can make you do. Slide, swing, climb, invert your body and hang upside down, etc. After igniting your man's imagination, crawl toward him and end your show with a final kiss. Lick each of his lips, suck on them, and then slide your tongue inside his mouth.

· Whip It Up Kiss ·

Have you been a bad girl or boy? You need some "love taps" to be taught a lesson. Put your partner across the knee and give them a light spanking. Pull them up and sit them across your lap. Keep tapping their behind while you kiss them. This kiss will have them crying for more.

• Cuffed Kiss •

Handcuff your partner to the bed and make them a prisoner of your sweet loving. While they are restrained, arouse them mercilessly. Suck and bite him in places that have them bucking like a wild horse. Kiss them on the lips and caress the sides of their body, lightly brushing the tips of your fingers on their skin. When their close to the edge, take off the handcuffs and let loose.

Blindfold Kiss

. . . .

Lay your partner on the bed and blindfold them. This kiss is all about erotic, sensory exploration. Choose a bunch of your favorite kisses from this book and let your partner experience what each one feels like. Take your time with each kiss so that they can feel the strokes of your tongue and the press and suction of your lips. Being blindfolded will heighten every sensation and will allow them to feel every kiss in the depths of their soul. They're body will be heaven bound.

. . . .

Silky Kiss

Tell your partner to close his eyes and run a silk scarf along his body. Alternate with soft kisses that tease and invite. The texture of this kiss is voluptuous, delicate, and sensuous. The feeling is simply exquisite.

Vibrator Kiss

While you're pleasuring your girl with hot lip and tongue action, use a vibrator to arouse her down south. As her body twists and jerks in pleasure, keep those kisses coming. The effect of this double stimulation will have her head spinning and sparks ricocheting off her body.

High Heel Kiss

When your hear your man's keys rattling in the door, welcome him home wearing your birthday suit and a pair of "come sex me" pumps. You're one hot mama, so strut your stuff with your killer walk and get your man's libido cooking. When you finally take a seat, tell him to take off your shoes. Let him kiss your feet and toes to get the party started.

Lingerie Kiss

Dazzle your man with some racy lingerie. Flaunt your sexy parts and make him desire you. Seduce him with your risqué kisses and lace undergarments. While kissing him, take his hands and guide his fingers along your breasts, torso, and pelvic area. The combination of sweet kisses and the feel of your body under lace will definitely get your man in the mood.

Lasso Kiss

Capture your lover in a chair and tie their hands behind their back. Give them all kinds of kisses, starting with their feet and working your way to their lips. You're in total control and when they're on the brink of exploding, pull back. Arouse them again, but this time take your lover over the edge with your magic lips.

Orgasmic Kisses

～ Seesaw Kiss ～

If you're in the mood to turn things up a notch, try riding your partner as you kiss. Sit with your legs open. Let your partner sit in the space between your legs, with their legs outstretched over yours. Rock back and forth, like you're on a seesaw. When you go forward, your partner should lean back. As you move together in a steady rhythm, give each other kisses.

G-Spot Kiss

While your man's boner is hitting your G-spot, double your satisfaction with his tongue tickling your palate. In the throes of passion, your mouths gape open, your breath is heavy and hot, and your tongues are like a dog's, wagging and licking in delight. At this point, you don't have a brain, your animal instinct takes over and your sexed-up body has a mind of its own. There's no restraint with this kiss. Just let your lips and tongues go buck wild while you climax.

69 Kiss

Giving and receiving kisses at the same time on each other's intimate parts is wicked fun. Ease into this kiss by teasing with your tongues, increasing stimulation. Lick, suck, and kiss each other, varying the pressure and pace, until you reach orgasm and explode.

Treasure Kiss

This kiss is all about exploration. As you set out to find your lover's treasure, let your tongue and lips explore different parts of their body. Don't get lost on the way; your final destination is their sexual gems. Before your discover them, let your lips and tongue pave a magical path of pleasurable sensation.

Tantric Kiss

There is no beginning or end to this kiss, just prolonged intimacy and sexual fulfillment. Create an atmosphere that puts you both in the mood for sexual play. Dim the lights, play soft music, or light incense. Take the time to caress and massage each other's bodies, awakening your desires. Explore the taste of each other's mouths and linger in the heat of your breaths. The final act is not sex, so push the boundaries of lip and tongue exploration.

Ballsy Kiss

Your man's Johnson usually gets all the action. This kiss gives lip and tongue service to his lonely balls. Lick, slurp, suck, and kiss his nuts. Begin at a slow pace, progressively working up a sweat, and then slowing it back down again. He'll be at your mercy.

· *Kinky Kiss* ·

Combine a hot kiss with some kink. Anything that rocks your sexual boat—role playing, dressing up, acting out fantasies, or fetishes—will add intensity to this smooch. It's not for the shy at heart, but for the bold and daring who seek intense sexual pleasure.

• Frisky Kiss •

This kiss is for playful lovers. You can do it anywhere—on the bed, under the covers, on the floor, on the table, in the shower, on the living-room couch. Make your kisses playful. Embrace your partner while your frisky hands tickle, tease, arouse, and ignite other parts of their body. Have them laughing, moaning, and screaming in passion.

Tease Kiss

The sole objective of this kiss is to drive your partner crazy. Angle your head and come close to your sweetheart's face. Look deeply into their eyes and then gaze at their lips. Lick your lips and give your partner's lips a quick stroke of your tongue. Pull back. Look into their eyes again and then focus on their lips. Lean close to their face and when your lips almost touch, pull back again. Each time your lips approach, increase your lip action progressively, pulling back each time until you satisfy their hunger and give them a full French kiss.

• *Lotus Kiss* •

This kiss is a very intimate and makes you and your lover feel as one. Sit cross-legged on the floor and seat your woman on your lap, wrapping her legs around your waist. Place your hands on her shoulders. Stare into each other's eyes. Share sweet kisses, suck on each other's lips and tongues. There's no rush to this kiss. As you kiss deeply and your crotches press against each other, let your passions unleash.

Carte Blanche

Diabolical Kiss

This kiss is merciless, the kind that takes your partner prisoner and never lets go. From the moment you give this kiss, there's no turning back. You must go all the way until you and your partner collapse in each other's arms. Start this kiss on the most sensitive body part on your partner. Your lips work hungrily to arouse them immediately. Once unleashed, passion cannot be abated. It's completely diabolical.

Swing Kiss

A hammock can become a cozy love nest for the sweetest kisses. The close proximity of your bodies, a cool afternoon breeze, and blue skies above create an irresistible romantic atmosphere perfect for smooching. While your bodies rock to a lulling sway, put your heads together, facing each other. Rub your noses together, share tender kisses, and whisper sweet nothings. Enjoy your afternoon of romance.

· Giddyup Kiss ·

This kiss is for all the cowboys and cowgirls who like to add flavor to their love life. While bucking and riding your partner in the throes of passion, bend down and pucker up at the same time. This kiss takes some practice, but once you get the rhythm, the feeling will have you neighing until climax.

Treasure Hunt Kiss

Set your partner on a treasure hunt around town. Guess who's the treasure? You! Give him clues where he can find you. Maybe the place has romantic significance for you or a special meaning in your love story. At the end of the treasure hunt, you'll be waiting for your Sherlock with a kiss well worth his efforts!

• *Garter Kiss* •

Stimulate your man's imagination in your sexy lingerie. As he sits on the bed, watching you strut your stuff, spark up his desire with your seductive charms. As you slink toward your man, prop your leg up on his lap and let him unfasten your garter. Slowly, he peels off your stockings, kissing and sucking your leg until it's completely off. Drop that leg back to the ground and prop up the other one. Très sexy!

• Hanky Panky Kiss •

If you're feeling a little daring, steal a moment of hanky panky in an elevator or train, in a public bathroom, or in a dark movie theater. Let your hands roam in desirable places and share a deep kiss. Get your hair mussed up and your lips wet. This kiss is relatively quick but effective.

• *Spanking Kiss* •

While your lady is in control, straddling her man, give her plump humps some love taps to rev up her pace. As she picks up her speed and her desire climbs, smack her booty a little harder. Make sure you're attuned to her bodily response to your spanking. As she's about to go crazy, get up and give her some more love taps as you slide your tongue in her mouth. She'll explode in your arms.

• No Hands Kiss •

Can you resist touching your partner when a kiss sets you on fire? This kiss challenges your sexual will power. Give your partner a slew of hot kisses, one after the other. No hands, please. The trick is to only use your greedy lips to excite your lover's libido. Keep those lips puckered up and see how long your partner will be able to keep their hands off you!

Bite Kiss

Lay your lover's body across the bed. You have their entire body to feast on. Give them soft bites all over. Start with their hands, feet, arms, and legs, saving the torso and intimate parts as the cherry on top. Make sure the bites are light, just hard enough to get their sexual juices flowing.

Panting Kiss

This kiss gives your lover a delightful preview of the main course. Kneel down in front of your partner. Slowly undo their pants and kiss their stomach, pressing your lips into their soft, cushiony flesh. Keep heading south, tug at their undies, and kiss the hairy padding covering the jewels. Change course and zip or button up your partner's pants. Stand up and give them a last kiss on the lips. That should get them panting for more.

Special Tricks

— Cigar Kiss —

Get close to your partner's face. Your noses should be almost touching. In your sexy voice, tell them to stick their tongue out. Adjust your head position and suck on the tip of their tongue. Suck a little bit harder, progressively taking their entire tongue in your mouth. As you keep pulling on your lover's tongue, remember that saliva control is key in keeping your lover turned on and wanting more of this kiss.

～ *Lip Combo Kiss* ～

This kiss is two-in-one. Kiss you lover's top lip only. Lick and take it into your mouth. Suckle on it. Now, move on to their bottom lip and repeat. Alternate between the top and bottom lips, keeping a steady pace. The trick is never to let your hungry lips cling to both of your lover's lips at the same time.

Slow Motion Kiss

What's your all-time favorite kiss, the one kiss that makes your sweetheart swoon in your arms? Give your chéri(e) that one special kiss in slow motion. Prolong the ecstasy, the pleasure, the sensation, allowing them to savor your kiss from the moment they feel your breath until well after your lips part.

Pouter Kiss

Mad about something? This kiss will make it all better. Kiss your partner's bottom lip. Tease it with your tongue and give it tender kisses to make their troubles melt away. If you've done this kiss right, their bottom lip will no longer be in a pout.

Feather Kiss

This kiss barely grazes your partner's supple lips, yet it gives them a rush of sensation. Wet your lips, and then your partner's. Brush your lips gently against theirs, left to right, up and down. Your wet mouths slide and touch just enough to send tingles down your lover's spine.

Deep Throat Kiss

This kiss is for those lovers who can't get enough of each other's love. When your lips touch, it's magnetic. You want more and give more. Locked in an embrace, your desire is greedy. Your tongues twist madly and reach far into each other's mouths, wanting more. If you could swallow your partner's mouth whole, you would!

Breathless Kiss

This is a marathon kiss, a make-out session for the record books. Plan a romantic evening at home with your baby. Settle in the love seat and start making out. This kiss creates such an intimate connection, and there are days when your lover needs more kissing than sexing. Just keep smooching and smooching until you're out of breath and saliva and your lips are numb.

Horizontal Kiss

Give a fresh twist to kissing your partner in the horizontal position. Lie on the floor or your bed, faces together, upside down, and bodies in opposite directions. Even though your heads are opposite, your lips should be aligned. Kiss each other in this position until you pull away and head to more imitate parts.

• Creole Kiss •

This kiss is a delightful mix of two or more kisses, but all uniquely your own. This kiss can be inspired by the mechanics of the different kisses in this book, but essentially it's distinct enough to be different. You've learned many tricks and tips thus far. Let your imagination overflow and your passion abound!

• Tongue Twister Kiss •

This kiss calls for gymnastics of the tongue. Twist your tongue around your partner's. For this kiss to feel real good, it's all about the pacing and staying in sync
with your partner. Change the speed, the direction, and keep the spit to a minimum. The feel of two slippery tongues dancing round each other gets you hot and
wet in intimate places.

Chapter Eight:
Lights, Camera, Kiss!

Kisses That Capture Magical On-Screen Moments

Couples with Sizzle

Casablanca Kiss (Ingrid Bergman and Humphrey Bogart)

"Kiss me. Kiss me as if it were the last time." Who could forget this scene when Ilsa Lund (Ingrid Bergman) declares how much she loves Rick (Humphrey Bogart). There's a foreboding in her voice, a part of her that somehow knows that the war will get in the way of their love. It's such a vulnerable moment between these two lovers. They look deeply into each other's eyes, their hands clinging together, and she pleads with him to kiss her one last time. Bogart delivers and it's one of the most romantic scenes on the silver screen. What kind of kiss would you give your partner if it were the last time? Get creative and knock your partner's socks off!

To Catch a Thief Kiss (Grace Kelly and Cary Grant)

One of the most seductive moments on the silver screen is the fireworks scene in this movie. Cary Grant's character, John Robie, meets his love interest, Frances Stevens (Grace Kelly), in her hotel room. She's a knockout, wearing an angelic white strapless gown. She suspects Robie to be a notorious cat burglar and wears a diamond necklace around her neck to get him to admit to it. Frances spreads her seductive charms thick, and it's not the diamonds he can't resist, but her. John tells Frances that they both know the necklace is fake. She responds, "Well, I'm not." John dives in for a kiss. Seduction is sexually powerful and a great lure for kisses that will crackle and pop.

Gone with the Wind Kiss (Vivien Leigh and Clark Gable)

The sparks between Leigh (Scarlett O'Hara) and Gable (Rhett Butler) pop off the screen. In a scene after her second husband's death, Rhett asks her to marry him in a playful manner. He tells Scarlett that he's a real man, of the right age, not a boy or an old man, in other words, types that Scarlet was used to. When she mentions Ashley, her unrequited love, he silences her with a kiss, one that no man had ever given her. Scarlett admits her desire to faint, obviously overwhelmed by such an impassioned kiss. She discovers real desire and the power of a kiss when done right. Give your partner a kiss that will make them weak in the knees. Remember, it just takes one great kiss to open the floodgates of our desires. Priceless!

Rebel Without a Cause Kiss (James Dean and Natalie Wood)

In one of the tenderest moments on screen, Judy (Natalie Wood) tells Jim (James Dean) all the reasons why she loves him. They are settled on the floor in front of a fire, Jim on his back, Judy on her stomach nestled next to him. As the scene progresses, her lips inch closer to his. As he feels her proximity, Jim's mouth parts and he turns his head to receive her kiss. On a cold, dreary winter day, get cozy and warm with some intimate time with your partner. Tell your sweetheart all the reasons they turn you on and make you hot. After your smoking confessions, they'll be offering you just about every part of their body to kiss.

The English Patient Kiss (Ralph Fiennes and Kristen Scott Thomas)

The sex interlude between Count Almásy (Ralph Fiennes) and Katharine Clifton (Kristen Scott Thomas) during the Christmas celebration is so erotic that words would have only been an intrusion. When they steal a forbidden moment together, their passion is a blazing fire. As the tune of Silent Night plays in the background, Almásy pins Katharine against an open cupboard, glances down at the body he is about to devour, takes off her corsage, and she unzips the side of her dress as an offering. He slips his hand inside to pull her closer to him. The scene gets spicier when he slips his hand under her slip to fondle her. After, she straddles him, their lips lock in a steamy embrace, part, and he slides his thumb into her mouth. Katharine sucks on it hard until, unable to contain her passion, her mouth opens, her lips searching again for his. You too can steal some time away with your lover and recreate the same sexual electricity. If you feel you're about to combust from all the lust inside, grab your partner, find a somewhat secluded place, and get it on standing up.

Titanic Kiss (Kate Winslet and Leonardo DiCaprio)

The chemistry between Rose (Kate Winslet) and Jack (Leonardo DiCaprio) is electrifying in Titanic. The scene when they make love for the first time in a car being transported on the ship is intensely erotic. Before they make love, Rose asks Jack to take her to the stars, and he does just that. She kisses his fingertips and tells him to put his hands on her. They recline in a steamy embrace. When the car is completely fogged up, and they reach the heights of their passion, they seal their tryst with two kisses. As Jack trembles in Rose's sweat-laced arms, they kiss once on the lips, and then she kisses him on the forehead with Jack collapsing on her bosom. Try rocketing to the stars in the backseat of your own car. Start with some hot and heavy loving and end with some kisses for a safe docking!

Unfaithful Kiss (Diane Lane and Olivier Martinez)

Never before has a carnal/fatal attraction been so palpable on-screen than between adulterous housewife, Connie (Diane Lane), and suave Frenchman, Paul Martel (Olivier Martinez). Their attraction sizzles in every scene they're in together. When they're about to make love for the first time, he lays her on the bed and caresses her stomach, rests his palm on her crotch to feel her heat, slips his finger in her skirt, stroking her pelvic area. Connie is shaking uncontrollably. She can't resist, but wishes she could. She knows she's losing the battle and is sliding into hell. When she finally surrenders, her kisses are animalistic! Even when your partner is about to explode from all their desire, take it nice and slow with erotic caresses, slow kisses, and deep sucks. When the beast is about to roar, let it rip!

Mr. & Mrs. Smith Kiss (Brad Pitt and Angelina Jolie)

The brawl scene between John Smith (Brad Pitt) and Jane Smith (Angelina Jolie) is one of the most passionate interplays between two characters. Dressed in a sexy black dress with high heels, Jane holds her own and fights her husband like a man. They're fighting to kill, destroying everything in their path, and shedding each other's blood. The fury comes to a climax when the fight comes to a standstill and they're pointing artillery in each other's faces. This is a breaking point for Jane, and they both drop the guns, grab the backs of each other's heads, their lips smashing together for a passionate kiss. This leads to some sizzling lovemaking. Be a lover, not a fighter. Make love, not war. Instead of fighting, enjoy a night of explosive kisses. Take it from room to room, your passion, instead of fury, causing havoc in your home.

The Bridges of Madison County Kiss (Meryl Streep and Clint Eastwood)

The four-day love story between Francesca Johnson (Meryl Streep) and Robert Kincaid (Clint Eastwood) is one of the most romantic stories ever. Their attraction becomes undeniable and Francesca falls in love with Robert. In one scene, when he goes over to Francesca's house for a formal dinner date, they dance in each other's arms, savoring the smell and skin contact. Their lips are like magnets and their mouths draw nearer and nearer. Their kiss is timid at first, their lips barely touching, taking time to fully meet and lock. It's such an intimate moment, the prime emotion between them being love, not lust. Let your heart do the kissing and not your libido. Kiss like you're discovering each other for the first time. Moments like this are always magical.

Twilight Kiss (Robert Pattinson and Kristen Stewart)

The impossible love between vampire, Edward Cullen (Robert Pattinson) and mortal, Bella Swan (Kristen Stewart) creates great sexual tension between these two characters. When they share their first kiss, we see that even a vampire is weak against the pull of the flesh. During one of his nightly visits to Bella's bedroom, he tells her that he's always wanted to try one thing. He asks her to remain very still and slowly moves in for a kiss. Bella reciprocates and they grab each other and Edward falls on top of her in a hot embrace. Quickly sensing the danger, Edward uses all his willpower and force to tear himself away from Bella's lips and arms. Would you have the same willpower? Could you resist the sweet taste of your lover's lips, the swell of your desires, the heat rising between both your bodies in the hush of the night?

Unforgettable Romance

~ Love Story Kiss ~

This is one of the great on-screen love stories. Jennifer (Ali MacGraw) and Oliver (Ryan O'Neil) give us an emotional performance as they fight to be together, only to be torn apart by a cruel twist of fate. They're from two different worlds, yet their love brings them together. In a poignant scene when they're walking across campus in the rain, Oliver tells Jenny that he thinks she's scared of caring, of risking her heart. Jenny finds the courage to admit that she cares and finally offers her heart to Oliver. They embrace, Oliver holding her head with both hands. Their kiss is the beginning of their love story. Declarations are best sealed with a kiss. After pouring your heart out to your special person, offer them a kiss that speaks volumes of the emotions inside.

• Rocky Kiss •

The magic of a first kiss is beautifully portrayed by Adrian (Talia Shire) and Rocky (Sylvester Stallone). She is an exceedingly shy, thirty-year-old virgin, and he's an uneducated, small-time boxer. Alone, the two are outcasts in society, but together, they're transformed. When Rocky convinces Adrian to come up to his apartment, she's afraid, having never been alone with a man. Rocky's tenderness and compassion soon abate her fears and awaken her passion. He takes off her glasses and hat and really looks at her, complimenting her beautiful eyes. He asks her for one kiss and slowly embraces her. She can't resist and shyly reciprocates. They kiss again, and this time, they fall to the floor, giving in completely to their desires. Feeling desired by your partner is such a magical feeling. Recreate this kiss by taking the time to notice and appreciate things about your partner. Look deeply into their eyes, caress their face, touch their lips, whisper just how you feel, and give them kisses that show just how much you desire them. Creating this first level of intimacy is highly erotic.

• *White Palace Kiss* •

Middle-aged Nora Baker (Susan Sarandon) stumbles across a young grieving widower, Max Baron (James Spader), and they both unexpectedly find love with each other. They're from different sides of the tracks, not to mention different generations, and share few common interests. Their love becomes impossible to sustain, especially for Max, who has difficulty bridging their worlds. Nora runs off to New York, and when Max finally has the courage to love her in the way she deserves, he soon follows and goes to the restaurant where she works to win her back. Nora finally gives in. Charged with sensuality, she cocks her head back and tells him, "Honey, I got everything you need." He gets up from the table and gives her a passionate kiss, knocking over the table's contents to spread her on the table. He gets on top of her, continuing to kiss her passionately. Finally he pulls his coat over their heads for more privacy. Now that's a kiss that sweeps you off your feet. How daring are you? Give your partner a kiss in public that whisks them off their feet, too. No need to be shy, for love knows no boundaries.

• The Piano Kiss •

Sometimes, love blossoms in unexpected situations between two of the most un-likely people. In one of the most beautiful love stories, a mute pianist, Ada (Holly Hunter), and her daughter are sold into an arranged marriage by her father to Alistair Stewart (Sam Neill), a New Zealand frontiersman. However, it's his friend, George Baines (Harvey Keitel) with whom she ends up madly in love. Ada, unable to stave off her desire any longer, goes to Baines. She struggles with her emotions and doesn't let him know the reason for her visit. Baines orders her to leave, for he, too, suffers with his feelings, which he believes unreciprocated. Just as Ada gets to the door, she slaps him, and then hits him continuously, a sign of her inner turmoil. She suddenly stops and, ceasing her fight, drops to the floor. Baines bends down and they look into each other's eyes. They know they love each other. Aida gets up and they hold each other tight, caressing and kissing. When he kisses her for the first time, it seems as if their lips are two halves fitting together to form a whole. Their scene of sweet surrender is one of the most freeing and heartfelt. Try this kiss when your partner needs to be put in the mood for love. Give them kisses that will make them surrender, slowly, but surely, to your loving. Always start off slow and sensual, allowing their body to feel every sensation.

How Stella Got Her Groove Back Kiss

The shower scene with forty-year-old Stella (Angela Bassett) and Winston (Taye Diggs), her young Jamaican boyfriend, sizzles with passion. After a big argument, she joins him in the shower partially dressed. With warm water dripping down their faces, desire pounding through their body, and Winston, standing erect in all of his masculine majesty, Stella gently soaps down her lover's back. She turns him around, positions her head, and they kiss, their lips hungry for each other's love. They move their lovefest to the bedroom where they make passionate love. If you had a big fight with your partner, start making up under a hot shower and let the water release all your tension and your kisses melt your anger. Sexy kisses will soften your partner's roar and tame the beast in both of you.

• Pride and Prejudice Kiss •

Jane Austen's endearing Mr. Darcy (Matthew Macfadyen) and feisty Elizabeth Bennet (Keira Knightley) are finally united in an unforgettable sunrise scene. As Elizabeth takes a walk on the moors, she spots her Romeo through the dew-laden air walking toward her. Elizabeth can't take her eyes off him. When he approaches, he confesses his love and asks if she feels the same, having outright refused his first proposal in marriage. In a line that any woman would love to hear her man utter, Darcy says, "If, however, you're feelings have changed, I would have to tell you, you have bewitched me body and soul, and I love, I love, I love you, and I never wish to be parted from you from this day on." Elizabeth approaches and takes his hand, responding, "Well, then." She gives him one tender kiss on his hands, a gesture that clearly says, "I'm yours." Just as they look deeply into each other's eyes, the sun comes up between them. Darcy rests his forehead against hers and they both close their eyes. In the hush of the early morning hour, go for a walk with your beloved. It's such a quiet, intimate moment to feel the love and share sweet kisses expressing the claim you have on each other's heart.

Bridget Jones's Diary Kiss

Every thirty-something single girl knows that when Mr. Right comes along, you can't let him get away. When Bridget Jones (Renée Zellweger) and Mark Darcy (Colin Firth) share their first kiss, Bridget is standing in front of him in her panties, wearing only a camisole and a cardigan to shelter her from the falling snow and freezing cold. Offering her a new start, Bridget jumps into Darcy's arms and they share a mind-blowing first kiss in the middle of the street. Surprised by his technique, Bridget says, "Wait a minute. Nice boys don't kiss like that." Darcy, responds, "Oh, yes, they f***ing do," and gives her a second round of hot smooches. Classic! With all the skill and variety you've learned, show your partner that good boys or girls can be naughty, too! Wow them with a first kiss, but take them to the moon the second time around.

Brokeback Mountain Kiss

Ennis (Heath Ledger) and Jack (Jake Gyllenhaal) finally reunite after an unbearable separation following their sexual experience during a herding gig one summer. It's been four long years of longing and lusting, so when they're at last in each other's arms, their passions are uncontrollable. Ennis pulls Jack out of sight and pins him against an area next to the stairs. They both hold each other by the head and kiss passionately. Jake reciprocates, shifting position, this time pinning Ennis against a spot on the other side. Their reunion is a carnal one. Desire is an untamed beast that needs to be fed. A kiss becomes a feeding frenzy, licking, biting, and sucking on your partner's mouth and flesh.

The Notebook Kiss

The kiss between Allie Hamilton (Rachel McAdams) and Noah Calhoun (Ryan Gosling) is one of the most memorable rain-soaked kisses on the big screen. During a heated scene, in torrential rain, she asks him why he didn't keep in touch because their relationship wasn't over for her. She waited seven years for him. He responds that he wrote her 365 letters, one for each day. He shouts, "It wasn't over. It still isn't over!" Wasting no more time, he grabs the back of her neck and she opens her mouth wide even before his lips approach hers. She then jumps up, straddling him, and Jake carries her into the house, their lips still locked in a passionate embrace. They ram each other against walls, tearing their clothes off as they make their way to the bedroom. If you want some of this same sizzle, start off a hot session of lovemaking in the rain. Begin with a kiss, lips and tongue in action. As things get heated, run for shelter, jumping in bed, still soaked from the rain.

• Walk the Line Kiss •

June Carter (Reese Witherspoon) and Johnny Cash (Joaquin Phoenix) were soul-mates. In the middle of their duet "Jackson," Cash stops the song, unable to continue if June doesn't agree to marry him. He's madly in love with June and is not giving up on her. He pours his soul out to her in front of the entire audience, promising never to hurt her again. June finally agrees to be his wife, and Cash picks his woman up in his arms and gives her a kiss. Overwhelmed with happiness, he swirls her around. Women love to be serenaded. Enjoy a karaoke night out with your main lady. Surprise her with a song meaningful to your love story. Pour your heart out, belt out the lyrics, and at the end, give her a kiss that makes her yours forever!

Memorable Moments

From Here to Eternity Kiss

The forbidden kiss on the Hawaiian beach between Army Sergeant Milton Warden (Burt Lancaster) and Karen Holmes (Deborah Kerr), the cheating Army Captain's wife, is one of the most memorable. Wrapped in each other's embrace, waves wash over their bodies while they kiss. Karen rises and runs away from the shore, collapsing on her beach towel. Milton follows and falls to his knees, bending to kiss her again. As their lips part, she stares up at him, her eyes dreamy and full of lust. She says, "I never knew it could be like this. Nobody ever kissed me the way you do." A great kiss can seduce, make you fall in love, light your fire, express so many emotions, or make you lose your mind. How does your partner rate you?

When Harry Met Sally Kiss

Harry Burns (Billy Crystal) rushes through Manhattan on New Year's Eve to a party to find Sally Albright (Meg Ryan). He can't wait to tell her that he loves her and wants to spend the rest of his life with her. She rejects the idea, but eventually tells him that she loves him, too. They seal their declaration of love with a kiss, oblivious to the festive crowd around them dancing to "Auld Lang Syne." Lost in your partner's kiss, time stops and no one else in the world exists. Despite the bustle of a crowded street or the cramps of a small, tight space, share a deep kiss and be swept away.

Ghost Kiss

Molding wet clay was never as sexy as depicted in the famous pottery-making scene between Sam Wheat (Patrick Swayze) and his wife, Molly Jensen (Demi Moore). Sam sits behind Molly while she molds a phallic-looking piece of pottery, the sensual tune of "Unchained Melody" setting the mood for some hot loving. Wet clay drips through their interlaced fingers as they try to erect the object. Their hands slip and slide against the object and caress each other. Sam gives Molly irresistible kisses at the back of her head. She can't resist and turns to kiss him. The scene is so erotic and gives so much fodder to the imagination. The feel of different textures on your hands or on your body intensifies your desires and adds excitement to your kisses and sexual play. Pick your favorite texture and don't be afraid to get dirty while lip-locking with your sweetheart.

An Officer and a Gentleman Kiss

When graduate trainee Zack Mayo (Richard Gere) walks through the grit and dirt of a paper factory, clad in his sparkling white naval officer's uniform, to whisk his love interest, Paula Pokrifki (Debra Winger), it's one of the most romantic, "knight in shining armor" moments. Zack surprises Paula with a kiss on the back on her neck. She turns around, and Zack gently holds the side of her face and kisses her. Paula wraps her arms around him and he picks her up, twirling her around. They share repeated kisses. Finally, he carries her out of the factory in his arms. After a hard day's work, plan to pick up your chérie from work. Surprise her with deep kisses that announce a long night of passion.

Legends of the Fall Kiss

The rugged Montana landscape provides the beautiful backdrop for the doomed love between Susannah Fincannon (Julia Ormond) and Tristan Ludlow (Brad Pitt). Although betrothed to the younger of the Ludlow brothers, Samuel, who is later killed in World War I, it's untamed Tristan who brings out her deepest passions. Their chemistry is undeniable, and after a dispute with his older brother, Susannah runs outside after Tristan. He grabs and kisses her, and, with no hesitation, they surrender fully to their desires. Sometimes, a particular setting helps bring out our wildest fantasies and hidden desires. Take time away with your partner in a place that makes you feel primitive and in touch with your rawest emotions. This is a time to try the most daring kisses in this book!

• The Last Samurai Kiss •

In an intimate scene that couples beauty and sensuality, Taka (Koyuki) dresses Captain Nathan Algren (Tom Cruise) in her dead husband's Samurai armor before he goes off to fight. Never before has putting on a man's clothes sparked such desire and quiet longing. From the moment she pulls off the sash holding his kimono to put on the battle suit, she makes love to him through her touch. Taka has grown to love Algren and it shows in the way she dresses him. Her touch and caress speak the truth of her heart. At one point, tears well up in her eyes, for she knows that he might very well die. They stare intensely at each other and share a pure, simple kiss. After that, she goes behind him and wraps her arms around his waist, resting her head just above his shoulder. What a feast for the eyes! Try recreating the same intimacy and igniting your man's desire by putting his clothes on. If you're touch is as magical as Taka's, your kisses won't be as pure and you'll be soon be taking his clothes off!

• *Spider-Man Kiss* •

The kiss between Mary Jane Watson (Kirsten Dunst) and Spider-Man (Tobey Maguire) is one of the hottest kisses in the rain. She thanks Spider-Man, who is hanging upside down in front of her, for saving her yet again from danger. She asks, "Do I get to say thank you this time?" She reaches for his mask, but he says, "Wait." Mary Jane pauses, but starts to peel down Spider-Man's mask until his wet lips are exposed. She gives him one of the hottest on-screen smooches ever— slow and deep, sucking on his lips. The kiss ends with their mouths open, feeling each other's breath. This kiss is easily achieved horizontally and is quite pleasurable. If you can do it vertically, you're a master smoocher!

· Bodyguard Kiss ·

A goodbye kiss is sometimes the most erotic and enduring. So much emotion goes into it because of the separation from a loved one or the uncertainty or certainty of never seeing them again. Rachel Marron (Whitney Houston) catches sight of her lover and ex-bodyguard, Frank Farmer (Kevin Costner), and shouts "Wait!" as her plane is about to take off. The plane stops, she emerges and runs into the arms of Frank. The camera spins around them as they share a marathon kiss, their lips never parting. It's a classic. The next time you have to say goodbye, make sure your kiss makes your baby want to come back to you!

• Jerry Maguire Kiss •

When Jerry Maguire (Tom Cruise) returns home to get back his wife, Dorothy Boyd (Renée Zellweger), he stumbles in the middle of her divorced women's support group. In front of all her friends, Jerry pours his heart out and declares his love for a stunned Dorothy. "You complete me," he says. Dorothy interrupts his speech, telling him to just shut up. In one of the most endearing lines on the big screen, she says, "You had me at 'hello.'" They run into each other's arms for a tender embrace. Sometimes, love hits you over the head immediately. You meet someone and you just know they're the special one. Don't be afraid to let your kiss reveal your true emotions. A fitting kiss needs no words to express what's in your heart.

Pirates of the Caribbean: At World's End Kiss

During a ferocious sea battle, Will Turner (Orlando Bloom) asks Elizabeth Swann (Keira Knightley) to marry him. Quickly, they turn to the captain Barbossa (Geoffrey Rush) to marry them. In the midst of fighting they say their wows. The captain can't finish pronouncing them man and wife and orders them to just kiss. In the middle of a raging sea, pouring rain, artillery, swords, and gunfire, they kiss passionately, swept away by their love. A meaningful smooch during an otherwise chaotic time and/or place can create an intimate niche against all the craziness.

A Streetcar Named Desire Kiss

The kiss between husband and wife, Stanley (Marlon Brando) and Stella (Kim Hunter) is one of the steamiest of the silver screen. He shouts her name several times at the bottom of the stairs, "Stellaaaa," and despair fills his voice. Stanley's sexual pull is obvious on his wife and she gets up, almost possessed, and slinks down the stairs. Stanley kneels down and awaits Stella on his knees. He has a tough, brutish exterior, but it hides an irresistible sensuality and sensibility. When Stella gets to the bottom of the stairs, she runs her hands through his hair and bends over to caress the full length of his back. He cries, "Don't ever leave me, baby," and picks her up. They kiss passionately as Stanley carries her into their house for a night of hot sex. Keeping a healthy sex drive begins with a passionate kiss. The skill and intensity of your lip action lets your partner know that they still drive you crazy!

• 9½ Weeks Kiss •

In one of the many erotic scenes in this movie, Elizabeth McGraw (Kim Basinger) is about to enter the kitchen when her lover, John Grey (Mickey Rourke), tells her to stop. She's dressed in a long white robe and white socks. He gets behind her and tells her that he wants her to close her eyes and slide down on the floor. She executes. The sounds in the kitchen begin to turn her on. In front of an open refrigerator, John feeds her all different kinds of food. He starts with a black olive, which he puts between her teeth, and he then follows with maraschino cherries, strawberries, champagne, spiral pasta, Jell-O, a jalapeño pepper, and milk that she gulps down, letting it fall on her chin, to calm the burn on her tongue. He shakes carbonated water and opens the cap showering her between her legs and in her face. To top off her feeding frenzy, he asks her to stick out her tongue and pours honey on it, and then pours it over her legs. He spreads the sticky liquid over her thighs and ends with an epic tongue and lick down. You have to try this one at home in your kitchen!

· The Lover Kiss ·

The relationship between the young French girl (Jane March) and the older aristo-cratic Chinese man (Tony Leung Ka Fai) is a feast of carnal pleasure. One morning, as the French girl arrives at school, she notices the Chinese man's car parked out-side. She approaches. His breathing becomes heavier. She places her hand on the window and he follows it. She draws nearer, and they stare intently at each other. She bends down, closes her eyes, and slowly presses her lips against the window. He, too, closes his eyes and parts his lips as if he's receiving the kiss! The sexual magnetism between these two characters is electrifying. As she pulls away, you can see in his eyes and body language that it's a painful separation for him. Her lips didn't even touch his, but you could tell that he felt every part of her window kiss. Does your kiss have the same effect on your partner?

• Fatal Attraction Kiss •

The chemistry between Dan Gallagher (Michael Douglas) and Alex Forrest (Glenn Close) is one of the most sexual and portrays the weaknesses of the flesh. They meet and are in instant lust. They spend a night on the town, which leads them into her elevator ripping at each other's clothes and hard-core sexual play. Their kisses are ravenous, primal, and insatiable. These kind of raunchy kisses lead straight to the bedroom and end in complete fireworks!

• Dirty Dancing Kiss •

Sexy dance instructor Johnny Castle (Patrick Swayze) and seventeen-year-old, Frances "Baby" Houseman (Jennifer Grey) sizzle on the screen with a budding romance and hot dance moves. It's a summer of discovery and exploration in which dancing ignites Baby's passions. During a visit to Johnny, Baby confesses that she's afraid to leave his room and never feel what she feels with him. She invites him to dance. To the tune of "Cry to Me," their body movements flow together perfectly in a sensuous rhythm. She caresses his naked torso, kisses his neck, and smells his skin. She's the one leading that dance until he shifts gears and takes off her shirt. He kisses her and dips her backward, taking the reins. Spend a night with your favorite jams and let the combination of music, touch, movement, and kisses give a spark to you and your lover's passions.

Basic Instinct Kiss

• • •

Police detective Nick Curran (Michael Douglas) and sexy mystery writer Catherine Tramell (Sharon Stone) have explosive sexual tension between them. When she's brought into the police station one day for questioning, she destabilizes an entire group of detectives with her charms. In one of the most erotic, infamous scenes on the big screen, she crosses and uncrosses her legs, revealing her bare crotch! Everything about Catherine seduced every man in that interrogation room, from the way she moved her body or positioned it, to her simple smile or set of her eyes. Use your seductive powers to lure your man to your lips. If you've excited him enough, you'll get a set of kisses that will make your libido rage!

Dangerous Liaisons Kiss

• • •

The scene of surrender of the devout and virtuous Madame de Tourvel (Michelle Pfeiffer) to the philandering Vicomte de Valmont is one of beauty. She gives up everything she believes in and ends up in Vicomte's bed. Responding to yet another one of her refusals, he threatens suicide and bids her farewell. When she tries to stop him, he pulls her to him and she surrenders in a slow, deep kiss. He carries her to the settee and she tells him that she could not live either if she didn't make him happy. "No more refusals. No more regrets," she says. How long can we resist true love and our innermost desires? When Madame de Tourvel finally gives up her struggle, abandoning herself to her lover, her kiss is sweet capitulation.

She's Gotta Have It Kiss

Nola Darling (Tracy Camilla Johns) prepares for a night with one of her lovers, Jamie Overstreet (Tommy Redmond Hicks). As a sensual jazz melody floats through her room, she lights scented candles all around her bed, transforming it into an altar. Her lover pulls her down on the bed for hot lip and body smooches. Nola's kisses are freeing, uninhibited. She likes to give pleasure as much as she receives it. She likes kissing and caressing her man's flesh just as much as she likes having sex. The golden rule is, "Kiss others as you would have other kiss you!"

Thornbirds Kiss

Meggie Clearly (Rachel Ward) has been in love with Father Ralph de Bricassart (Richard Chamberlain) for most of her life. However, he has always refused her advances, choosing God over her. During a weekend getaway on Matlock Island, father Ralph joins Meggie on the urging of his superior to face his temptations. Ralph finally succumbs to his love for Meggie and when they consummate that love, it's one of the most explosive love scenes on the small screen. When he runs after her on the beach, he pulls her down and smothers her in kisses. Meggie and Ralph's passions are literally unleashed on each other. Ralph is on fire and kisses Meggie's lips and body with such intensity and passion. This is the kind of kiss that never stops and leads to all night loving.

• *Atonement Kiss* •

Two young soulmates finally admit to their love in a touching scene of love and lust. As Cecilia (Keira Knightley) tries to explain to Robbie (James McAvoy) what she's been feeling, tears stream down her face. He asks, "Why are you crying?" She looks at him in surrender and says, "Don't you know?" He confesses to her that he does know and, pinning her against the library bookcase, gives her their first kiss. They stare into each other's eyes and kiss a second time, timidly at first, and then more passionately. She's wearing a long, stunning, emerald green dress with a plunging back line, which resembles the color of a lush Garden of Eden full of temptation. When they become more intimate, they suddenly stop at a pivotal moment to declare their "I love yous." They resume their coitus with soft kisses. Their kisses are sweet and tender, passionate and erotic, a great mix of smooches to declare one's burning love!

• *Body Heat Kiss* •

Ned Racine (William Hurt) and Matty Walker's (Kathleen Turner) tumultuous affair sizzles on screen. The sexual chemistry cuts like a knife. In one of the sexiest scenes in the movie, Matty is standing in the foyer of her house looking at Ned outside. She's wearing an irresistible red hot, short skirt and the desire is apparent in her eyes. Ned can't resist Matty, but the glass door is locked. Like a man possessed, he takes a chair to smash it open. Matty stands waiting as he rushes toward her and scoops her into his arms. They kiss and caress each other hungrily. Their kisses intensify and soon they are on the floor and Matty's begging Ned "to do it!" Have you ever desired someone so much that you would break through any obstacle or travel anywhere to get to them. When you do, you kiss them with all your might. This kiss will definitely raise your body temperature and drive you wild.

· Purple Rain Kiss ·

When the Kid (Prince) brings his love interest, Apollonia (Apollonia Kottero), back to his house, it seems more like a love den than a place to crash. His room is dimly lit. The tape of the cries of a woman, mimicking the groans of sexual pleasure, permeates the space and creates an erotic atmosphere. When the Kid gives her a first kiss, it's a simple peck. His kisses become longer, more assertive, as they abandon themselves to each other. Standing behind her at the foot of his bed, he strokes her pelvic area and brushes his lips against her neck and face. Dressed to get it on, Apollonia is wearing red string panties and a black bustier. He changes sides and kisses her more passionately. The expression of desire takes all kinds of kisses!

• Pretty Woman Kiss •

Have you ever been fondled and kissed on top of a piano? Sounds simply sinful, and it is. This is one of the hottest scenes between Edward Lewis (Richard Gere) and Vivian Ward (Julia Roberts). Vivian joins Edward in the lounge of the hotel in which they're guests. He's at the piano and she stands in front of him, leaning on the keys. She's wearing a long white bathrobe and a black slip underneath. He opens the robe, picks her up, and sits her on top of the piano. He caresses her hair and grabs the back of her neck, drawing her lips near. Vivian pulls away, refusing to kiss on the lips. Edward opens her legs to pull her closer, lays her down on the piano, and caresses her arched torso. He jacks her slip up and kisses her stomach. Even if you don't have a piano, you don't have to miss out on this kiss. A kitchen counter or table will suffice!

Eyes Wide Shut Kiss

One of the steamiest husband-and-wife love scenes takes place in front of a mirror. Alice Harford (Nicole Kidman) is completely naked in front of her dressing mirror table. Only wearing her glasses, she pulls off her earrings one by one, swaying to the fitting tune of "Baby Did a Bad Bad Thing!" Her husband, Bill (Tom Cruise) joins her, and they stare coyly at each other's reflections. He kisses her neck and caresses her breast. She turns to face him and they kiss. Alice takes off her glasses and watches their reflection in the mirror as her husband kisses her neck. A mirror heightens your passions times two! Having the image of you and your partner connecting in intimate ways reflected back to you is highly erotic. This is a sure turn on that will spark your fire.

From Dusk Till Dawn Kiss

There are many elements to seduction. A stare. Soft caresses. Pleasurable scents. Sexy wear. The way your body moves and shimmies. When the curtain opens to an audience of men, Satanico (Salma Hayek) walks out like she's about to bring the house down. All eyes remain on her, mesmerized by her sensuality. She's wearing a red bikini, a feather headpiece, and a cape. When she swings off her cape, a python is hanging around her neck. She starts her dance to the Chicano rhythms of a song called "After Dark." Every part of her body moves in sync with the snake. When the snake is lifted off her shoulders, she ventures into the audience, sashaying on the tables until she stops in front of Richie Gecko (Quentin Tarantino). She bends down and picks up a bottle of alcohol, pours it down her leg and puts her foot in his mouth, circling it around while he sucks on it. Then she pushes his head back with her foot. She balances on one leg and licks her alcohol-drenched shin. The final touch is when Satanico cocks her head back and takes a drink from the bottle. She bends down again, opens her mouth, draws near as if to kiss Richie, and pours the spirit into his mouth. Untouchable! Ladies, if you can dance like that and give such innovative kisses to your man, he'll be eating out the palm of your hand until death do you part.

• *Monster's Ball Kiss* •

In a sexually charged, animalistic scene, Leticia (Halle Berry) and Hank (Billy Bob Thornton) push the limits of human desire. Devastated by loss and guilt, they find solace in sex to relieve each other of their great pain. With the buzz of alcohol lowering some of her inhibitions, Leticia begs Hank to make her feel good over and over again. The desperation in her voice is chilling. They claw, pinch, grab each other's flesh, get down and dirty, and share deep kisses that take some of their pain away. Total abandonment can take you for a wild ride. To start your journey, give your partner kisses that will allow them to let go and fly away with you.

• Kama Sutra Kiss •

Maya's (Indira Varma) seductive skills make her the prince's (Naveen Andrews) favorite courtesan. During one of her visits, she pulls off the bed sheet and slowly climbs on top of him. She caresses his chest and, working up his torso, gives him playful love bites. The prince is already moaning. She moves on to his lips, sucking the bottom one, then the top, adding little kisses in between. She takes her time, making him want her even more. When her lips brush against his, his mouth is hungry for her love. Slow, artful kisses awaken the flesh's erotic sensations and frees your partner's desires.

Damage Kiss

Dr. Stephen Fleming (Jeremy Irons) and Anna Barton (Juliette Binoche) lose themselves in a spiral of passion that consumes them. Their desire for each other is so strong that it follows no reason. In one scene when he has her pinned to the floor, their lips barely touch, but they're like magnets so drawn to one another. Their lips are parted, but they never fully kiss, for the proximity is enough. This kiss combined with hot lovemaking is a toe-curling experience!

Desperado Kiss

Carolina (Salma Hayek) and El Mariachi (Antonio Banderas) share steamy smooches that will add fire to your lovemaking. She holds the sides of his face and puts his entire chin in her mouth, sucking on it. Then they move on to the horizontal kiss, and as El Mariachi moves down her body in the opposite direction, Carolina licks him. Their tongues continue to lick and kiss each other until she falls back in his arms. Love sessions are doubly orgasmic when you partner gets as much lip and tongue action as this hot sexy loving.

Match Point Kiss

Nola Rice (Scarlett Johansson) and her lover Chris Wilton (Jonathan Rhys Meyers) still have not had enough of each other and continue their frolicking as they kiss up the stairs of Nola's apartment building. When they get inside Nola's apartment, the lovers turn the heat up. Chris pushes her against a wall and they kiss passionately. Nola pulls his tie off, blindfolds him, and spins him around. Quickly, from behind, she unbuttons his shirt while he opens her pants. Blindfolded kisses and sexual play multiply the sensations and take you to the depths of your passion. H-O-T!

Chapter Nine:
Harmonious Kisses

Kisses to Bump and Grind To

Oldies that Never Stop Grooving

"At Last" Kiss (Etta James)

This is the romance classic of all time. Played at every occasion in celebration of love at last found, couples cling to each other in an amorous embrace, slowly rocking to the sultry lyrics belted out by the great songstress Etta James. This song plays to the tune of L-O-V-E and this kiss feels like paradise. The skies are blue. Your sweetheart's love is a thrill you've never known and it's yours at last. The kisses are sweet, blissful, harmonious, and simply divine.

"Love Me Tender" Kiss (Elvis Presley)

Love makes you bashful, vulnerable, gentle—your heart busting with emotion. Who could have sung these tender moments better than the King, the great teddy bear of love? Hold your sweetheart closely, give them tender kisses on their face, sometimes simply resting your lips lightly on theirs. As you declare your love to your one and only, take them in your arms and give them a kiss that makes them yours till the end of time.

"When a Man Loves a Woman" Kiss (Percy Sledge)

You're head over heels, don't know your name, can't live without her in love. When your Juliet is near, your eyes sparkle, your heart beats to the cadence of love, and your soul stirs within. Her kiss is magical and you savor each one. The feel of her lips makes you dizzy and her tongue in your mouth is enough food to feast on for a lifetime.

"Me and Mrs. Jones" Kiss (Billy Paul)

Some kisses are just forbidden, too risqué for daytime; yet they are so addictive. You can't get enough of your Mrs. and she's got a thing goin' on that will never make you leave. Her kiss is like a drug and when your lips touch, she turns you into an insatiable beast. After each kiss, you already ache for the next one. She sucks your lips in a way that makes you lose your mind every time.

"I Just Called to Say I Love You" Kiss (Stevie Wonder)

You've got the kind of love that makes an ordinary day special. No need for celebrations, declarations, or grandiloquent demonstrations of love. A simple kiss is all that's needed to show your honey pie the love overflowing in your heart. Any moment of the day is perfect to grab your partner and smooch—a loving, toasty smooch that says, "I love you."

"You Are So Beautiful" Kiss (Joe Cocker)

Finding someone who is beautiful in every way is a special thing. Their love is a remedy for every ailment. The way Joe Cocker's raspy voice croons about the beauty of his lady merits a kiss that will brand yours with your love. It's passionate, wild, steamy, incredibly satisfying. It's everything you've hoped for and need.

"(You Make Me Feel Like) A Natural Woman" Kiss (Aretha Franklin)

• • •

A natural woman gets the kind of love that turns her inside out, makes her feel alive, and gives her a reason. One of your kisses can make her feel like a natural woman— loved, desired, impassioned, giddy, determined . . . putty. Set her entire body on fire and let your lips and tongue unlock the deepest part of her femininity. After your kisses, she'll know what the Queen of Soul is really singing about!

"Just a Be Close to You" Kiss (Commodores/Lionel Richie)

• • •

When you finally find that special person, your love seems infinite and forever stretches before you like the yellow brick road. You only want to nest with your significant other, savoring their smell and feeling their skin close to yours. Love struck, you spend hours kissing, petting, canoodling, and lazing in each other's arms. Your kisses linger and last a long time. Each one makes you both yearn and burn for each other's love.

"The Long and Winding Road" Kiss (The Beatles)

There are those kisses that you never get out of your system. Kisses that have left an imprint on your lips and a sweet taste in your mouth. A great kiss is memorable, never forgotten, like a toe-curling French kiss, or a tingling neck kiss, or a sinful oyster kiss. Each time your lips meet, you want that one special kiss that always gets you hot and heavy and keeps your running back for more.

"Brown Eyed Girl" Kiss (Van Morrison)

Love is playful. It makes you feel young and carefree. You want to hold hands and run in the rain. Skip down the street or laugh out loud. Sing and dance. Put on Van Morrison's catchy tune and boogie with your girl or guy. It's these kinds of sweet moments that are memory making. You'll look back and say, "We danced like crazy, kissed like hell, and made love like rabbits!"

Jazzing It Up

"My Funny Valentine" Kiss (Frank Sinatra)

When O' Blue Eyes sings this song, lovers hold each other tight, close their eyes, and lose themselves in a slow melody filled with memories of everlasting love. Your love has come a long way and your baby is still the sexiest of them all. This tune is melodically sexy. It plucks your heartstrings and makes you want to spend the entire night kissing your Valentine under the stars.

"Unforgettable" Kiss (Nat King Cole)

When Nat King Cole's velvety smooth voice intones that you are unforgettable, it puts you in a dreamy mood. Your arms wrap around each other's necks, foreheads touching, and your feet shuffle from side to side. Your lips touch and you close your eyes. Suddenly you feel light as a feather, your feet leave the ground, and you're flying high above. If you could touch love it would feel like that.

"Concierto de Aranjuez"
Kiss (Miles Davis)

• • •

If ever there was music that embodied seduction, sensuality, and lust, it's Miles Davis' interpretation of Joaquin Rodrigo's best-known composition. The texture of this song is silky. The notes travel deep inside you and the rhythm hypnotizes your body in a slow trance. This song is especially made for an afternoon of slow love, slow kisses, and slow sucks! Pleasure yourselves all day in these dulcet vibes.

"The Girl from Ipanema"
Kiss (Stan Getz)

• • •

When you close your eyes and listen to this song, a soft breeze passes by, your feet sink in warm sand, and the lap of the ocean coddles your memories. Just sit back and enjoy the soothing samba rhythms of this jazz melody. Love waifs through the air and keeps you nestled in your partner's arms. Your smooches are smooth and continue even after the music stops playing.

"My One and Only Love" Kiss (John Coltrane)

Play this song at night when you and your loved one are under the sheets, skin to skin. This song is hypnotic and intensely romantic. In the hush of the night, in your moonlit love nest, hum to the sound of love. Your kisses feel like fire, transmitting all of your bodies' desires and the love that's burning in your heart. This song will rock you well into your lovefest.

"If I Should Lose You" Kiss (Nina Simone)

The legendary Nina Simone's version of the possible loss of love is hypnotic. Her voice is wistful and emotional, completely vulnerable. She's pouring her heart out to her love, feeling her despair when she sings, "stars would fall from the sky, leaves would wither and die," if her love was lost. Who could resist such a declaration of love? It merits a reassuring kiss that shows your woman that you're not going anywhere.

"Time After Time" Kiss
(Chet Baker)

This classic jazz standard is a dreamy hymn about the endurance of love. With time, your love grows stronger and remains fresh and new. This is a dance for old souls, lovers united through thick and thin. As the great Chet Baker's vocals sweep you up in sweet nostalgia and memories, dance the night away in your sweetheart's arms, sharing sweet kisses.

"The Look of Love" Kiss (Dusty Springfield)

What does love look like? Dusty Springfield's sultry vocals sing about desire and longing for the person loved. It's a look that gives you pause, a touch that makes you shudder, a kiss that makes your insides burn. This song is sensual and feels as smooth as velvet. Light some candles, play this tune, and enjoy a lustful night in your boudoir. You have the entire night to show your partner just how long you've desired him. Smother him in kisses and never let go.

"My One and Only Thrill"
Kiss (Melody Gardot)

Moments of love and dizzying passion are special. It's all consuming and holds you prisoner until your desire is satisfied. When your lover is your one-and-only thrill, nothing else matters in that moment, but the feel of their skin, the taste of their mouth, and their sweet, tender loving. The bluesy tone of Gardot's voice is a fitting melody to focus on, giving your partner long caresses, deep kisses, and all-night loving.

"You and I Kiss" (Michael Bublé)

This is a great song for a first dance at your wedding. It's a beautiful tribute to a life of love and partnership that begins for you and your partner. Bublé's smooth, jazzy voice gives this song a sensual crooner feel, expressing many of the emotions of newlywed couples embarking on a new life together. At the end of this song, one simple kiss is required to seal the deal!

Ballads for All the Lovers in the House

"Let's Get It On" Kiss (Marvin Gaye)

Ooh! Ooh! Some things just can't wait! Such as desire, passion, and love. These emotions are selfish, impatient, ardent, and restless. When Marvin Gaye croons, "Stop beatin' round the bush, and let's get it on," what are you waiting for? Put this jam on and get to loving right away. The first kiss is instant, your mouths part, and your tongues explore each other's mouths. The temperature is hot from the beginning and the fire crackles until the very end.

"Feelin' Like a Woman" Kiss (Millie Jackson)

When you have a man that makes you feel your feminine prowess, he has a hold on you forever. Your feet feel light, your hips roll with a swing, your arms flutter like wings, and your heart rages with fire. You wear his love like it's your own skin. His touches and loving have you feeling alive, and each of his kisses strips you of any inhibitions, unlocking your deepest passions! Millie Jackson's raunchy lyrics and heartfelt tone declare it best, "Feelin' like a woman makes me feel free to be so much of a woman with you!"

"Weekend in New England" Kiss (Barry Manilow)

You've been missing your significant other, longing for their lips, smell, and arms around you. Your strong yearning will finally end. Your eyes meet, the emptiness subsides, and excitement floods your entire body. Their kiss pumps life into you, makes your blood flow, and reignites the flames of love. At the moment your lips touch, all the love inside overflows and fills your kiss with intensity, fire, urgency. Reunited finally, you're with swept up in a kiss that never ends, holding each other again.

"You're the First, the Last, My Everything" Kiss (Barry White)

When the charming Maestro with the Velvet Voice croons his steamy lyrics for his special lady, it's one heck of a declaration of love. His tone caresses and makes you hot even before your clothes and panties come off. This kiss immediately puts you in the mood for all-night loving. If you were kissed one last time, this kiss would be it. You feel everything with this kiss. Your lover's heart beating, the spark in his touch, the fire of his passion, and his love burning through his body!

"She's Like the Wind" Kiss (Patrick Swayze)

•••

This is a perfect song to cap off a night with your special lady. When you get back home, kick off your shoes, put this jam on, and ask your lady for a dance. Keep the lights off and just let the melody and the smooth texture of Swayze's voice surround you. In the dark, your senses are heightened. You feel your lady's breath against your face, the warmth of her body close to yours, and her desire for you mounting. As you go round and round, kiss her softly on the lips and savor the taste of her.

"She" Kiss (Elvis Costello)

• • •

If you want to remind your lady just how special she is to you, this song is a beautiful love declaration. Stripped down to just a piano melody, the message is simple. She's your love, your life, your everything. That deserves a special kiss, one that'll make her feel like the center of your life. Sit your woman down on your lap, and while this tune plays in the background, kiss her like she's the queen that rules your world.

"Sweet Love" Kiss (Anita Baker)

You're so in love that you feel no shame. Your man's sweet love will make you scream his name from the rooftops. Prepare a night of seduction for your Romeo and start the festivities off with this song. Baker's distinctive, jazzy voice will quickly turn the mood to love. Your kisses show your man just how sweet his love is. They're slow, deep, and wet!

"Do Me Baby" Kiss (Prince)

When the irresistibly sexy Prince growls, "Do me, baby," it's time to get down to business and stop playing games. This song is about letting out your desires and giving 100% of yourself to your partner. You gotta play this song on loop all night long. It'll layer your lovemaking with an extra special feel. Do as Prince says. Take your baby and kiss him all over. Let your kisses bring out all his desire and give it to him like you've never done before. If you're doing it right, your man should be very vocal. Ooh! Ahh!!

"No Ordinary Love" Kiss (Sade)

Your love is no ordinary love. The sensual, raspy voice of Sade feels soft and silky. It'll caress you both as you lie in each other's arms. This smooth rhythm is perfect for a hot-and-heavy session of canoodling, fondling, and making out. So, explore your partner's flesh and mouth and discover over and over again why your love is extraordinary.

"Turn Me On" Kiss (Norah Jones)

Your lips have one mission—to turn your partner on. Play this bluesy tune, setting the mood as your lover walks through the door. You feel daring and ballsy, and as the sensual tone of this song works through you, your desire awakens and sets you on fire. When your guy finally walks through the doors, stand up in all of your naked glory, sashay up to him, and kiss him like a hot and brazen mama!

Popping and Rocking

"Your Song" Kiss (Elton John)

Sometimes, the most beautiful words are so simply said. Without any fireworks or useless banter. This kiss is sweet and simple like this song, yet overflowing with emotion. This song is for those ordinary occasions, everyday moments of life together that feel special and everlasting. This kiss is spontaneous and given when the heart desires. Out of the blue, your partner leans over and gives you a dreamy kiss on the lips or hands that speaks a thousand words.

"Wonderful Tonight" Kiss (Eric Clapton)

In a crowded room or an empty one, you always feel wonderful, for you are loved by your one and only. This quiet melody is an ode to how simply wonderful love makes you feel. There's a bright light that never dims when your heart burns for your partner. When you get home from a night out on the town or a raving party, hold your partner still and kiss her on the forehead, eyelids, lips, and neck. Your kisses will let her feel all the wonder you feel inside.

"Open Arms" Kiss (Journey)

True love is naked and honest. Your heart gapes open, giving and receiving infinite love. When Steve Perry's soaring vocals sing, "Now I come to you, with open arms, nothing to hide..." you can't help but feel every word and emotion. Play this song over and over while you're wrapped in each other's arms, rocking slowly, your heads touching, eyes closed, and your lips brushing against each other's.

"I'll Stand by You" Kiss (The Pretenders)

Love is a mighty emotion. It makes you feel brave even when you feel weak. It gives you hope when you're sad. It opens a door when another one closes. Sometimes your partner needs to be reminded that your love is here to stay. This kiss is for those moments when fear, sadness, and loneliness need to be swept away.

"My Heart Will Go On" Kiss (Celine Dion)

When you're touched by love, it lasts forever. This classic song is an anthem for everlasting love. Love that defies time and place, life and death. Dion's powerful vocals sound ethereal, like a hypnotizing hymn of love. As you slip into bed with your beloved, play this tune of undying love. This kiss goes on forever, a marathon kiss that goes on until you fall asleep in each other's arms.

"Pour Some Sugar on Me"
Kiss (Def Leppard)

This rock anthem will get your lady pumped up and in the mood to pour sugar all over you! Get ready for a night of uncensored loving. Squeeze, tease, razzle, dazzle, suck, lick, bite. Nothing is off-limits when you've been craving for each other's hot loving. It's a night to remember, so get down and dirty to this classic that will keep you going well into the night!

"All I Want Is You"
Kiss (U2)

This beautiful love song starts out quiet, but by the end, it rages. It's the cry of man's burning love for the woman he chooses. All he wants is you. Nothing else holds its weight against his love. This kiss is your man's claim on you. Just like the tempo of this song, it starts out slow and timid, but progressively intensifies until calmed by complete satisfaction.

"Songbird" Kiss (Fleetwood Mac)

This song feels like the early morning hours, just before night takes flight of the Earth. It's quiet and whispers a sweet message of love in your ear. A piano melody coddles and caresses you both while huddled in your love nest. It's just as soothing as a bird's early morning song. This kiss is affectionate and delicate. It's a beautiful start to your day!

"You're Beautiful" Kiss (James Blunt)

• • •

Whether you're sick, tired, stressed, or feeling undesirable, your man's stare, touch, kiss, and loving all make you feel beautiful. When his lips touch yours, you feel special in every way. They way he outlines your lips with his fingertips, or sucks ever so slowly on your lips, or inserts his tongue deeply into your mouth . . . You feel his desire each time on his lips as they declare loud and clear, "You're beautiful!"

"Your Body Is a Wonderland"
Kiss (John Mayer)

• • •

This song is the perfect melody for an afternoon of carnal exploration in between the sheets. In a soft-spoken pitch that hides his sexual appetite, Mayer croons about candy lips, bubblegum tongue, many inches of flesh to explore and devour, and making sweet love in a rented room. This kiss is an all-over body kiss. It starts from the top of your head and ends at the tips of your toes. Lose yourself in the discovery. Discover and be discovered and put time at the backs of your minds.

Dance Mix

~ Rub-a-Dub Kiss ~

This dance style requires you to get close and cozy with your partner. As the boum boum of the drum machine pumps Jamaican rhythms into your body, grind to the beat against your partner's mid section. Romeo should hold onto your hips so he can feel the full effect. The music and the bump and grind of your sweetheart make you work up a sweat. The movements are sex on the dance floor. Your kisses should be spicy and each one should lure out the animal in you. When you turn around for a kiss, full tongue on tongue is required here!

Tango Kiss

This dance form is a work of art. Visually, it's a palette of all the colors of love—raw emotions, untamed attraction, passion, intensity, sensuality, sexuality, etc. and arouses at the most primitive level. With its impassioned movements and erotic style, lovers engage in a tug-of-war of love and lust. The sensual sounds of accordion, violin, guitar, and piano will add fire to your wild kisses and make you hungry for each other's love. When your partner snatches you in a close embrace, plant your lips on his with force. Your lips sizzle!

· Lambada Kiss ·

This sultry Brazilian tempo is made for lovers. The sensual spins and raunchy hip movements bait your man and tease his imagination. The sound transports you to the warm beaches of Brazil where your inhibitions drop and your desires take over. On a cozy evening, just as the sun is setting, play some of this hot-blooded music, and let your man take you for a spin. Show him some hip and booty technique, alternating with playful licks and provocative sucks that promise a night of untamed passion.

Salsa Kiss

This Caribbean and Latin American dance is all about the spicy flavor. Shoulders shimmying, gyrating hips, wicked legwork, and liberating moves. When a woman dances the salsa, she feels liberated, sexual, and desirable. It's a contagious and magical rhythm that gets the blood pumping and the passions flowing. Get your partner up on his feet and show him what this beat does to you. Your kiss—wet and wild—will be your ultimate love offering!

• Belly Dancing Kiss •

This art form, which focuses on erotic hip and pelvic movements, spins a web of irresistible seduction. The movements are so feminine and illustrate the divine power of the female anatomy to attract her mate. Be careful! Your man won't be able to take his eyes off your body as you sway your hips, twists your waist, and wave your hands through the air. Take your time leading up to this kiss. Hypnotize him with your bellybutton, and when he's completely under your spell, make him your slave with kisses, taking his tongue progressively into your mouth.

• Soul Kiss •

A combination of gospel music and rhythm and blues, soul music charges at you and enters deep inside, taking hold of the soul. It's naked emotion, intense feeling, and a testifying of our innermost emotions. To listen to a soul song is to travel across an emotional landscape. To experience a soul kiss is to journey to the depths of passion. When your lips touch to the gritty and heartfelt lyrics of an old soul tune, your bodies will melt and it'll feel like two souls kissing.

Disco Kiss

The days of the strobe lights, the spinning glam ball, the sweaty club goers boogying to an infectious electric sound in droves at Manhattan's famous Studio 54 may be over, but disco still gets us on the dance floor. In remembrance of the frenzied nights of dancing and seduction, get your partner up and shaking their booty. Lure them to you through your cool moves worthy of the greatest era of dance. This kiss is seductive and direct. It starts on the dance floor and ends in the bedroom.

Flamenco Kiss

With grace and precision, the dance of the flamenco is an emotional template. Each movement hits a nerve and reveals a deep emotion betrayed by sharp body angles and intense facial expressions. From the snapping of fingers, tapping of feet, quick turns, and body jerks, this Spanish, gypsy dance captures you visually and whisks you away on an emotive journey. This kiss resembles the fire, desire, jealousy, and passion in your heart. It's one of those kisses that's frank, to the point, with a touch of aggression.

Country Kiss

Country music is the soundtrack of sweet hopes and dreams, life's pains and struggles, love and heartbreak. The lyrics are tender and the melody is heartfelt just like this kiss. So, take your sweetheart in your arms, and put your head on each other's shoulders and rock steady. Love is a beautiful thing!

Ballroom Kiss

What mood is your love in? A sizzling mambo? A fiery tango? A diabolic Paso Doble? A jazzed lindy trot? A svelte and stylish foxtrot? Whatever the dance, choose a kiss that matches the desire in your heart. If you're feeling many things, express them in every way through your body and lips. Don't be afraid to use everything you've got. Passion is transmitted through the flesh!

Chapter Ten:
Globe-trotting Kisses

The Most Erotic Places to Kiss

Darling Cities

New York—Gotham Kiss

New York City is home to the most famous kiss in the world. Who could forget Alfred Eisenstaedt's iconic photograph of the sailor kissing a woman in Times Square on V-Day. Times Square is the heart of Gotham City. The bright lights, Broadway marquees, the endless cluster of skyscraper buildings, the constant bustle and excitement, the noise of steel and concrete, and the promise of champagne dreams and caviar wishes. Stand in the center of the city, bend your lady backward, and give her the longest smooch ever! Be passionate, be wild, and be free! Anything goes in the city that never sleeps!

Las Vegas—Sin City Kiss

A weekend in Sin City is just what Cupid ordered to add sparks to a dormant sex drive. As the Strip welcomes you, get ready to lose yourselves in the neon life of twenty-four-hour casinos, live entertainment, drunken fun, exotic dancers, and Elvis impersonators. This city calls for your raunchiest, hottest, most sinful kisses. Enjoy the ride, baby. And remember, what happens in Vegas stays in Vegas.

New Orleans—Mardi Gras Kiss

The two-day revelry of carnival rhythms, colorful parades, and festive crowds, provides the perfect atmosphere for a euphoria of kisses. Parade down Bourbon Street or in the French Quarter with your sweetheart in the unbridled excitement of the biggest party in the world. Let loose and overindulge in your kisses. They should be saucy and without inhibition in the frenzy of the feast just before the famine.

Honolulu—Aloha Kiss

Take a trip to paradise and let the Aloha spirit welcome you into this lush dreamland. Fronted by the Pacific Ocean and backed by the majestic Ko'olau mountains, Honolulu provides an idyllic setting, combining the energy and excitement of a cosmopolitan city and the tranquility of dreamy beaches. Spend your days cozying up in the sun or being one with nature. In this garden of Eden, the landscape should inspire innocent, tender, and passionate kisses. At night when the sun goes down and grown folks come out to play, the island's endless offerings of nocturnal pleasures should spice up those kisses and make you drunk on love.

Paris—City of Lights Kiss

Steeped in tradition, history, style, glamour, and pure chic, Paris provides an amorous atmosphere for lovers to get it on all around town. Winding lanes, cobblestone streets, and pathways lead to charming hidden pockets and coves that are seductive for wandering lovers. Historic neighborhood quarters, endless littering of cafés on almost every street, scrumptious gastronomy, and divine wines charm all your senses and sweep you into a romance for the storybooks. The City of Lights is actually the City of Love and Kisses, and every kiss is as passionate as the next Bisous!

• London—Royal Kiss •

In no other historic city landscape can you find such architectural and cultural novelty. To visit London is to visit the world. It's a Mecca for innovative architecture and design, a flourishing of the arts, the frenzy of pop culture, and the proliferation of enduring music. While on the cutting-edge of the twenty-first century, London's tradition and glorious past are pervasive in the city's cherished monuments anchored throughout the city. Buckingham Palace, Big Ben, the Tower of London, Georgian squares, luring narrow alleyways, and heaps of rollicking pubs will set the tone for your prince to take you on many journeys. All of your kisses, from gallant to raunchy, will be inspired by the ages.

• *Rome—Roman Kiss* •

Amore! Amore! Rome is a city that inspires love, friendship, and beauty. The Roman tourist wants to wander through the narrow alleyways and cobblestone backstreets to stumble upon the great historical relics or one of the city's charming cafés or delicious trattorias. There's no rush to do anything in this beautiful Baroque city, which is a feast for the eyes and palate. As you take time to savor good food, good drink, and good company, take time also for love. Rome is magical that way. It will deepen your love and add more passion to your kisses. Red-blooded kisses with a joie de vivre will be the main menu!

Vienna—Viennese Kiss

Vienna is the city of magnificent orchestras and delightful waltzes. During warmer times, music pulsates everywhere in this city, which is steeped in the great musical legacy left by some of their very own—Beethoven, Mozart, Schubert, Strauss, etc. The atmosphere of the city inspires romance and makes you long to be in the arms of your sweetheart, looking deeply into his eyes, swept away in a tender kiss.

Barcelona—Spanish Kiss

A constant flurry of architectural innovation, cultural activity, alluring nightlife, and seaside fun makes this busy Mediterranean port a perfect summer destination for letting your hair down. Get ready for a long party. Jam-packed bars, restaurants, and clubs, keep you and your honey hopping from one place to the next. The nocturnal buzz will appeal to the hedonist in you, so turn up your lip and tongue action to sizzle.

Cape Town
—South African Kiss

Cape Town is for the outdoor lovers. Nature lures you into her web in Cape Town, inspiring a romantic atmosphere for love under the sun. The majestic Table Mountain stands erect in the middle of the city while mountainous slopes, pristine beaches, fertile valleys, and vineyards occupy this beauty of a city. Hikes, strolls, drives, long walks, sunbaths, sailing, and a slew of other activities will keep you outdoors from dawn to sunset. Your kisses will be primitive, fierce, liberating, and oh so natural.

Amorous Destinations

Napa Valley —Vineyard Kiss

A weekend with good wine, good food, good relaxation, and good loving is just the retreat the doctor ordered. Drive through rows of vineyards nestled in Napa Valley, indulging in a feast of drink and food fit for a king and queen. The orchards, trees, and hills are such a charmer that they will make you stop the car to gaze at the beautiful landscape. During one afternoon, take a picnic basket, a corkscrew, and Napa's best. After your lunch for two, lie back and rollick in the valley, kissing and fondling against the fertile earth of the Napa region.

Côte d'Azur
—French Riviera Kiss

Take a drive through the French Riviera with your sweetheart and fall in love all over again. Clusters of charming French coastal villages wait to be explored. Dine in the elegant resorts of Nice, Cannes, St. Tropez, or Monte Carlo, reminiscent of the 1950s and 1960s heyday of the rich and famous; or take a whiff of the perfume capital, Grasse; or luxuriate on the many beaches of Fréjus and St. Raphaël. Life is good in the South of France. Nothing can resist the charm and seduction of the Riviera. Every variation of the French kiss is required on this trip to perk up your libido.

Islamorada (Florida Keys)—Sunshine Kiss

This group of six islands offers a lush tropical getaway for lovers, honeymooners, or anyone with love on their mind. Beachfront cafés, miles of white sand, and hot sun will help you relax and get in the right mood. Make this place your love haven. Walk barefoot, wear very little clothing, and pucker up every chance you get.

Caribbean—Tropical Kiss

The Caribbean is custom-made for romance. The sweet smell of ripe fruits; the sensual rhythms of calypso and reggae melodies; the beat of the African drums; the stretch of white sand beaches and breezy, turquoise waters; and magnificent sunsets make you languor in each other's love and warmth. All you want to do is kiss and make love, make love and kiss.

Minorca—Iberian Kiss

Minorca is a Mediterranean love nest. After Mallorca, it's the largest of the Spanish Balearic islands. Less frequented than the touristy Mallorca, Minorca can boast of untouched beauty and a bevy of beautiful beaches. You don't go to Minorca to party, but to kiss and make love. A favorite pastime on this island is taking long walks on the sandy beaches and paths. Between the beach and the bedroom, your kisses will linger.

Rio de Janeiro
—Brazilian Kiss

Leave your inhibitions at home, because this stunning Brazilian city will unleash your desires and stroke your libido. Rio is called the "marvelous city." Beauty is everywhere—the architecture; luscious topography; the people, representing every hue of the planet; and the sensual rhythms of samba and bossa nova. The city's pulse is found in the south where white sand beaches and deep blue waters bustle and hustle with residents. The passionate spirit of this city is infectious and will seduce you in unimaginable ways. Your kisses should be as sexy and intoxicating as this seductive city.

Fez—Moroccan Kiss

Considered the soul of Morocco, Fez is the oldest imperial capital. Get lost in the magical, old medina, which has thousands of narrow alleys brimming with life, sounds, exotic smells, delicacies and spices, colors, and products. Caught between the Middle Ages and the modern world, the preservation of this city is remarkable. After wandering in the medina, spend your Arabian nights in the architectural splendor of traditional Moroccan riads and dars in your sweetheart's arms. The exotic setting will slowly bring out in the animal in you.

Istanbul—Bosporus Kiss

Explore a labyrinth of alleys and back streets that take you on a journey between East and West, ancient and modern, and exotic and extraordinary. Istanbul is a city of contrasts, straddling two cultures, Europe and Asia, and a magnet for exploration and entertainment. The skyline is dotted with high-rise buildings, palaces, mosques, and historical sites. Busting at the seams of the city are cafés, bars, first-class restaurants, and nightclubs that will entertain any night owl. In such a place, one goes with the flow. You never know what you'll discover and experience when you let go. After taking in an orgy of color, sound, and sights, your lips should show no restraint. Let them be indulgent, passionate, and explosive!

Bali—Indonesian Kiss

One of Indonesia's 17,500 islands, Bali stands alone in its beauty and lush topography rivaling Eden. The island is a scenic tapestry of long stretches of magnificent beaches, dense jungle, rice paddies terracing the hillsides, and ancient Hindu temples. Peace and tranquility reign on the island. Nature and man are one. You can easily escape into the landscape from your bed. In paradise, your kisses enchant, surprise, and mesmerize.

Cyprus—Aphrodite Kiss

This Greek island nation in the Mediterranean has a distinct personality with its close proximity to Syria, Turkey, and Lebanon. Birthplace of the goddess Aphrodite, supreme goddess of love, beauty, and sexuality, Cyprus is the ideal setting and getaway niche for lovers. Rising from the foam of the waves off the coast of Cyprus, Aphrodite was known to dazzle everyone with her beauty, inciting powerful feelings of love and lust. It's no wonder that this beauty emerged from the waves of this island nation also known for its seductive natural beauty. Golden beaches, lush mountains, rugged coastlines, picturesque villages, medieval castles, and breathtaking views are a powerful aphrodisiac for lovers rekindling the flame. Under Cyprus' spell, your kisses will come from your innermost passions!

Romantic Bridges, Lover's Squares, and Favorite Haunts

Brooklyn Bridge (New York)

The Brooklyn Bridge is one of the iconic symbols of New York City. Connecting two of the most famous boroughs, the bridge has become a hotspot for lovers who enjoy the experience of walking across it hand in hand or gazing at the stunning New York skyline. Suspended over the East River, halfway between Brooklyn and Manhattan, in one of the greatest American cities, your kisses will be full of fervor and passion.

Magere Brug—The Skinny Bridge (Amsterdam)

Overlooking the Amstel River, this wooden drawbridge is one of the most beautiful bridges in Amsterdam. Originally its name reflected the narrow width of the bridge, making it impossible for two pedestrians to walk together. Renovations have remedied this problem, and lovers can snuggle alongside each other with no problem. The best time to canoodle on this bridge is at night when thousands of fairy lights illuminate it. The ambiance makes for romantic kisses. Besides your lover's wet lips and sexy eyes, it's a sight to see.

Pont des Arts (Paris)

This steel and wood bridge is only for pedestrians, aimless wanderers, and, of course, the strolling lovers. Linking the Institut de France with the Louvre, it crosses the Seine River, offering a beautiful view on each side. To watch a sunset from the Pont des Arts, the last of the sun's rays hitting the river, is simply breathtaking. Bask in the Parisian view from this bridge and let those intense sensations fuel your kisses.

Piazza Navona Square (Rome)

Considered as one of the most beautiful of Rome's squares, a stroll around this lively area feels like a walk through history. The festive atmosphere is a magnet for many to just hang out and soak it all in. Outdoor cafés and restaurants line the perimeter of this square, and musicians and artists offer entertainment and art. The three fountains are the square's main attraction, the largest being the Fountain of the Four Rivers. As you sit on the edge of the fountain, let your lips lock in a long embrace in the midst of all the beauty and excitement unique to Rome.

Leicester Square (London)

Leicester Square is the heart of London's famous entertainment district—the posh West End. Many people gravitate here to go to the theater, catch a movie, or dance the night away in nightclubs. The square is a great starting point for a date night in the area. There's a small garden in the middle of the square where you'll find a marble statue of William Shakespeare. In homage to the poet and playwright who wrote one of the greatest love stories of all time, share a kiss with your Romeo or Juliet.

• Red Square (Moscow) •

Red Square is also known as the beautiful square, since the word "krasnaya" means both "red" and "beautiful" in Russian. Upon visiting the square, the majestic beauty and historical splendor are immediately imposing. Images of military parades, the walls on the Kremlin, and the architectural wonder and elegance of St. Basil's Cathedral remind you of thousands of years of history and culture. A visit to the square at night is breathtaking. Stand in the middle with your beloved and look up at the stars. Your kiss will be nothing less than magical.

Favorites

— *Park Kiss* —

Take your sweetheart to your favorite park. It's a day for romance and for reconnecting. Spend the day holding hands, talking and listening to each other, taking a canoe or carriage ride, having a picnic, and/or walking barefoot in the grass. Most of all, share sweet kisses, slow and deep kisses, and kisses that will create a new level of intimacy. Nature has a way of allowing us to reconnect with ourselves and one another. Kisses are sweetest when two lovers are in sync!

Jazz Joint Kiss

Nietzsche once said, "Without music, life would be an error." Music is capable of bringing out every emotion inside of us, adding flavor and spice to love. Take your honey to your favorite jazz bar and connect through music. Jazz is an orchestra of instruments—saxophone, trumpet, bass, piano, drums, trombone, flute, tuba, etc.—the sounds of which wrap around you like silk and seep deep inside your bones. Shimmy those shoulders, tap those feet, and let your body feel the rhythm. Your kisses will be sensual and seductive.

Café/Bar Kiss

Remember your first dates? The long conversations? The prickly sensations at the back of your neck? The nervous giggles? The pounding of your heart? The first kiss and the make-out sessions. If you can't remember your last date night, then this kiss is for you. Make a date night with your sweetheart and go out to the favorite bars, café's, or restaurants where you spent time together. Rekindle some of those burning feelings and kisses that helped the two of you fall in love.

Hotel Kiss

...

Check into your favorite hotel with your significant other, hang the "Do Not Disturb" sign on the doorknob, and order in room service for the weekend. Spend a weekend in between the sheets away from the kids, your life's constraints, and the rest of the world. Rediscover each other's bodies and your desires. There's nothing more erotic and satisfying than completely knowing your partner sexually. Start with your lips, tongue, and hands to get the party started. Hot. Hot. Hot!

Cozy Beaches

Pink Beach
—Harbour Island, Bahamas

More than three miles of perfectly pink sand beaches stretch across Harbour Island, making it one of the best beaches in the Bahamas. People from all over the world come to Harbour Island just to take a walk on this rare sand. The water is warm, the days sunny, and the nights balmy. The setting is ripe for love. Pink symbolizes sweetness, tenderness, newness, purity, femininity, and sexuality. Give your partner kisses that reflect the color pink.

Green Sand Beach
—Hawaii

As the rarest gems are the best hidden, this gem of a beach is hard to find. Located at the southernmost tip of the Big Island, Ka'u, it's in a very secluded area. It's a two-mile trek to access this beach, and then it's a rugged climb down. After all the effort, don't think about taking a cool swim, for the waters are too turbulent. The sight of the green-tinted sand is enough to reward your efforts. The color comes from rare olivine crystals. The color green symbolizes life, nature, the environment, vigor, energy, freedom, and possibility. Each of your kisses should feel like the emotions associated with each of these words.

Punalu'u Beach—Hawaii

The beautiful black sand of Punalu'u beach is one of the top black sand beaches in the world. The lava granules feel soothing against the skin and the sand is warm like a blanket. It's also the only beach where you can see sea turtles sunbathing close to the shore. Spend the entire day luxuriating on the smooth sand with your beloved. Black symbolizes power, depth, mystery, the wild side, and the unknown. You've learned lots of tips and tricks in the book. Give your lover the most surprising kisses to mystify them.

Red Sand Beach (Kaihalulu)—Maui

Kaihalulu is one of the rare red sand beaches in the world. It's a hidden gem on the island of Maui and is in relative isolation. The hike to get to this beach is a dangerous one. The path is steep, narrow, and slippery. The sand gets its deep reddish color from the crumbling cindercone hill surrounding the bay. Many people consider the sight of this beach enough. The green ironwood trees, the rocky lava sea wall, and the red sand are breathtaking. Red symbolizes all the colors of love—passion, desire, your heart, and excitement. Pucker up and plant some red hot kisses on your lover's lips. Red drives you wild!

Moshup Beach—Martha's Vineyard, Massachusetts

Moshup Beach is a hidden gem on Martha's Vineyard. Tucked under the more popular Gay Head Cliffs, a national landmark, the swarms of people never venture all the way to this beach. Soft white sand stretches across the beach, offering a serene, off-the-beaten-path landscape perfect for lovers. The warm waters, the beauty of the landscape, and the remoteness of the beach entice couples to just lie on the sand, snuggling and smooching in each other's arms.

Matira Beach—Bora Bora, French Polynesia

Considered Bora Bora's finest, the powdery white sand of this secluded beach offers a quiet paradise for lovers. Off Matira Beach is a sandy-bottom lagoon perfect for snorkeling, diving, or swimming. The quiet atmosphere, the pristine beach, and the heavenly landscape offer a love nest where you can lip-lock and get it on all day long. Nature calls for no inhibitions!

Coronado Beach —San Diego

Sparkling sand stretches hundreds of yards wide on this beach, which makes it ideal for spending the entire day smooching under a beach umbrella as the sun sets on the horizon over the Pacific Ocean. This beach is considered the crown jewel of San Diego and is picture-perfect fun under the sun. When your smooches get too raunchy for the rest of the beachgoers, take your lovefest to the nearby elegant, Victorian-style Hotel del Coronado where you'll cap off the night with fireworks!

Grace Bay Beach—Turks and Caicos Islands

...

Sparkling turquoise waters and bleached white sands cover twelve miles of this beach located on the northern coast of the island. Considered the Caribbean's finest beach, Grace Bay's tranquil, picturesque setting allows couples to recharge their batteries and rekindle flames. It's perfect for a wedding, declaring one's love, or just puckering up under the sun or in the ocean.

Ocracoke Island Beach—North Carolina

• • •

Accessed only by ferry, this beach is considered among the last of the pristine beaches along the Atlantic. Part of the sprawling Cape Hatteras National Seashore, a wide expanse of sand, clear waters, miles of sand dunes and marshlands are part of its natural beauty. This barrier island beach is never crowded and offers an ideal laid-back atmosphere to watch the sunset, walk hand in hand, or share tender sweet kisses.

Plage de Pampelonne —St. Tropez, France

•••

This historic nude beach is considered one of the hot spots in the St. Tropez area. It's referred to as decadent for the beautiful white sand and naked sun worshippers basking all day in the golden rays. Couples looking to spice things up would feel at ease letting it all hang out in this fun and trendy crowd. So, if you'd like to do as the French, take it off and enjoy the sun, the water, and the glamour. Your kisses will sizzle!

Irresistible Sites

Iguazu Falls (Brazil/Argentina)

Straddling the Argentinean and Brazilian borders, the magnificent Iguazu Falls represents the power and might of nature. With 275 terraced falls stretching over two miles of the Iguazu River and powering down from a height of 269 feet, the Falls are wider and taller than Niagara Falls. The thunderous roar of the water vibrates through you while the powerful gush makes your heart beat faster. It feels commanding, masculine, and virile. Turned on by the forces of nature, connect with your partner, sharing kisses that reflect the roar of your heart and the force of your desire.

Grand Canyon (US)

Standing before the Grand Canyon, looking into a massive gorge carved more than a mile deep by the determined Colorado River, you can't help but marvel at the forces of nature. Taking in the 277 miles of breathtaking landscape and color, the billions of years of the Earth's geological history exposed, and the immensity of the untamed canyon is empowering. So many emotions come at once and flood our senses. Power. Inspiration. Passion. Determination. Seduction. Such emotions should infuse new life into your kisses. So grab your partner and give them one hell of a kiss!

Hot Water Springs (Dominica)

This little gem of an island is one of nature's best-kept secrets. Tucked away between the two French islands of Martinique and Guadeloupe, Dominica is well known among nature aficionados for its irresistible hot sulphur springs hidden. Many volcanic hot spots dot the island and allow for private romantic frolicking in bubbling warm water pools. Get naked with your sweetheart and enjoy nature's therapeutic water against your skin. It's said to be magical and will lure out your deepest desires. Your kisses are sure to create some volcanic activity of their own.

Li River (China)

To settle your eyes on the Li River is to be looking at an artist's painting. The scenery is a masterpiece. Originating in the Mao'er Mountains and continuing south to Wuzhou, the river flows for a 230-mile course, along which a scenic view of steep cliffs, green hills, caves, and farming villages decorate the landscape. The scenic river takes on different aspects depending on the weather. During sunny days, the water becomes a crystal ball reflecting the surrounding hills. When mist hovers around the hills on cloudy days, the atmosphere feels like a magical wonderland. The dreamy atmosphere will make you fall in love all over again and sprinkle your kisses with passion.

Taj Mahal (India)

The architectural splendor of the Taj Mahal has been adored and venerated since its construction in the seventeenth century. Its presence against the Agra skyline is imposing and unapologetic— like the love behind its inspiration. Grief stricken by the death of his third wife, Mumtaz Mahal, in 1631, the emperor Shah Jahan commissioned the building of the Taj Mahal. The palace is an architectural feat. Beauty is found in every ornate detail of the white marble structure, with its minarets, vaulted archways, and the famous marble dome mirrored in a long reflecting pool. The Taj Mahal stands as a splendid testament to love, which should inspire your kisses and make you a hopeless romantic.

The Pyramids
(Egypt)

The architectural prowess of the Pyramids of Giza reflects a glimpse of the greatness of Egyptian civilization. Considered the oldest of the Seven Wonders of the Ancient World, the skill and mathematical precision it took to build these pyramids are astounding. So much history is etched into these massive stone structures. One can only imagine the splendor of the original limestone gleaming in the sun. The pharaohs believed that death was just a continuation, a beginning to our journey into the next world. This idea reminds us that love never dies. The spirit of the wise pharaohs inspire sweet, long kisses to remember for a lifetime.

Eiffel Tower (Paris)

Paris' magnificent symbol of beauty, industrial chic, and engineering achievement towers more than 1,000 feet over the city and weighs approximately 10,000 tons. Whether you're standing on top with a plunging view of the Ile de France or at the bottom looking up into its arched base, this iconic tower resembles a massive phallic structure embodying strength, stamina, and endurance. Millions of lovers flock to this monument venturing to the very top to experience one of the most breathtaking aerial views of Paris. At night, lights illuminate the entire iron lattice tower, highlighting its unrivaled beauty. The feeling is overwhelming, sparking passions and igniting love. Your kisses are on fire!

The Empire State Building (New York)

One hundred and two stories tower over Manhattan, making this Art Deco skyscraper a New York City landmark. It's the tallest building in the state of New York and is considered one of the seven Wonders of the Modern World. Observatories on the 86th and 102nd floors offer panoramic views of one of the most impressive cities in the world. Floodlights illuminate the top of the building at night in symbolic colors, making this tourist attraction even more irresistible. Indeed, it has become a meeting place for lovers from around to the world to declare their undying love to each other and seal it with the most passionate kiss.

Venice Canals (Italy)

Venice is a labyrinth of canals, bridges, pedestrian alleys, magnificent palaces, churches, etc. in which couples can get lost. Although the traditional Venetian boat is the gondola, it's used mostly by tourists and has become a favorite romantic experience for couples. Lovers are serenaded by their gondolier while they experience the elegance of this seductive city. The magic of Venice rekindles your fires and inspires the sweetest kisses.

The Alhambra
—"The Red One" (Spain)

The beautiful Alhambra is Moorish architecture in all of its splendor. It is one of the best-conserved Arabian palaces of its time and dominates the Grenadian skyline. Dating from the thirteenth and fourteenth centuries, this palace-fortress consists of three parts: Alcazaba, the fortress; Alhambra, the royal palaces; and Generalife, the summer palace and gorgeous gardens. The name Alhambra means "the red one" in Arabic, referring to the color of the fortress walls. The reddish tint heightens the exotic feel of the setting and the erotic esthetic of the design. Your kisses are urgent and smoking hot!

About the Author

Janete Scobie was born on the Caribbean island of Dominica and grew up in New York City. Longing to experience life overseas, Janete moved to Paris, France where she spent nearly a decade. Her travels eventually led her back to the States where she wrote her first novel, *The Seeds of Green Mangoes*. A bona fide Francophile, she divides her time between New York City and France. She is currently working on her second novel.

About Cider Mill Press
Book Publishers

Good ideas ripen with time. From seed to harvest, Cider Mill Press brings fine reading, information, and entertainment together between the covers of its creatively crafted books. Our Cider Mill bears fruit twice a year, publishing a new crop of titles each spring and fall.

Visit us on the Web at
www.cidermillpress.com
or write to us at
12 Port Farm Road
Kennebunkport, Maine 04046